# The Big C

## "C" for CHRIST

not cancer, not covid,
Nor Any Other Painful Small 'c's in Life

Aurora Ileto Opiniano

**A 31-Day Devotion**
**with Testimonies from**
**Ordinary people**
**with One Extraordinary God!**

# The Big C – "C" for CHRIST
## A 31-Day Devotion with Testimonies from Ordinary people with One Extraordinary God!



Cover & Book Designed by

TRUTH Communications Media & Publications

TruthCommunications.org



Published by TRUTH Communications Media & Publications

www.TruthCommunications.org

Printed in Canada



ISBN 978-1-7776796-0-6

## Dedication

Dedicated to my family
especially my grandchildren,
who is my inspiration in life;
to honor and remember
Wilma, my best friend,
Who encouraged me
to write this book;
to my friends, who have gone
to be with the Lord;
and to all those who are at war
with cancer, covid, or other painful
circumstances in life.

---

Above all,
this book is dedicated
To the Lover of my soul,
My Lord and Savior Jesus Christ!

# CONTENTS

# INTRODUCTION

The battle against cancer is real.

The war on the unseen virus continues.

News about war and catastrophic events around the world is happening.

Is it possible to have peace amid panic and chaos? Will there be joy when you are struggling due to sickness and other devastating circumstances?

The answer is YES and AMEN!

This 31-day devotional book aims to give hope and encouragement through God's Word. The personal testimonies of those who experienced the power and love of the Living God were included to show that God answers prayers and that all things are possible with Him. The big "C" comforts the weary, helps the needy, and brings peace amid calamity. The Big "C" supersedes the small "c"s, which is everything we do not welcome. To differentiate the big "C" from the small "c"s, the author decided to use lowercase for the small "c"s like covid-19 throughout the book.

Each day, after studying the Word of God, the Readers are encouraged to write their prayers, thanksgiving or adoration to the Lord. Reading the Book, meditating on His Word and lifting the requests and petitions to the Lord will draw us to a deeper faith in and understanding of the God of the Bible.

Every day, the unique Hebrew name of One True God, as mentioned in the Holy Book, will glimpse the true character of the Loving Father, the Creator of Heaven and earth, and the Great *I AM.*

***"Now may the God of hope fill you with all joy and peace in believing, that you may abound in hope by the power of the Holy Spirit."***
***Romans 15:13***

# DAY 1: THE GOD OF PEACE

***"Peace I leave with you; my peace I give to you; not as the world gives do I give to you. Let not your heart be troubled, neither let it be afraid."***
***John 14:27***

In October 2017, after several medical tests, I finally got the result. I have aggressive and advanced stage three breast cancer. With its size, I will have to undergo chemotherapy, surgery, and radiation. After briefly discussing with the Doctor, I headed home and walked to my car. I turned on the radio. This is what I heard:

***"Peace I leave with you; my peace I give you…"***

I felt His presence when He assured me through His Word that He would never leave or forsake me. He held my hand when I was afraid. He embraced me when I was discouraged through this painful journey.

I praise the God of Peace. He cares. He heals. He helps. He understands the pain. He will comfort you the same way he comforted me.

This is what Fae, my daughter-in-law, once wrote: "When we first found out Mama was diagnosed with cancer, our hearts broke. Many loved ones have fought difficult fights with cancer, so this was unwelcome news. During this season, our faith community and loved ones surrounded her with prayer like a fortified wall. The battle for Mama was not easy, but she was not alone. We were not alone. Our God embraced her and us with His tangible love and incomprehensible peace. Who finds peace in situations like these that seem so dire? In moments when unhuman peace envelops utter human brokenness, I am convinced God is real and very present to those who cry out to Him. Our emotions were real, Mama's pain was real, and our peace was genuine."

**Prayer:**

God, truly, You are the God of Peace. You are The big "C" (Christ), the Great Physician who heals those who are sick. You are the compassionate Christ who is bigger than cancer. I pray for protection over the health of my family, friends and all who read this book now and for the rest of their lives. I pray that those who are sick will receive healing, comfort and peace that passes all understanding. Thank You, YHWH Shalom!

***YHWH Shalom is a Hebrew name for God, meaning The Lord is Peace. It is one of many Old Testament names for God used by Gideon during his greatest distress. God promises that He will be with him in the battles to come.***
***Read: Judges 6:24***

**Lord, I pray for peace…**

________________________________________

________________________________________

________________________________________

________________________________________

________________________________________

________________________________________

________________________________________

In Jesus Name, Amen!

*"These things I have spoken to you, that in Me you may have peace. In the world you will have tribulation; but be of good cheer, I have overcome the world."*
*John 16:33*

*"… His name will be called … Prince of Peace"*
*Isaiah 9:6*

# Day 2: The God of the Angel Armies

***"For we do not wrestle against flesh and blood, but against principalities, against powers, against the rulers of the darkness of this age, against spiritual hosts of wickedness in the heavenly places."***
***Ephesians 6:12***

This is a battle - a fight to the finish. The Message version of Ephesians 6:12 says, "a life-or-death fight to the finish against the Devil and all his angels".

Wearing the full armour of God, I could see myself ready to fight the battle, not on my own strength. The God of the Angel Armies is ahead of me. He had already won the battle when He died on the cross, rose from the dead, and was seated at the Father's right hand. Around me are other soldiers of God geared up, praying for me and with me to win this war.

Cancer is a battle. Any sickness is a battle. The battle is not only physical but also financial, emotional, and spiritual battle. This is not only a struggle against flesh and blood but a war against the spiritual forces of wickedness whose goal is to steal, kill and destroy God's people. Winning this battle means fighting the good fight of faith – believing in God's absolute goodness, infinite wisdom and unfailing love.

**Prayer:**

Lord, You already won the battle! Thank You for being the Sovereign God who will sustain us in this long, tiring, and painful war. Almighty God, give us the courage to stand strong to fight the good fight of faith and finish the race. When feeling tired, weary, and ready to give up, hide us under the shadow of Your wings so we may find rest and peace as we claim victory over death. Let us not lose hope. You already won the war! May Your presence, protection, and power be upon those who are at war. Thank You, YHWH Sabaoth!

***YHWH Sabaoth - Lord of Hosts***
***The Hebrew name for God that declares God's reign over heaven and earth and all armies, earthly and spiritual***
***Read: Joshua 5:13-15;1 Samuel 17;***
***Psalm24:9-10; 84:3 and Isaiah 6:5***

**Lord, I pray to win this battle:**

______________________________________________________________

______________________________________________________________

______________________________________________________________

______________________________________________________________

______________________________________________________________

______________________________________________________________

______________________________________________________________

In Jesus Name, Amen!

*"The thief does not come except to steal, and to kill, and to destroy; I have come that they may have life, and that they may have it more abundantly."*
*John 10:10*

*"The Lord of hosts is with us…"*
*Psalm 46:7*

*"…I come to you in the name of the Lord of hosts, the God of the armies of Israel… for the battle is the Lord's…"*
*1 Samuel 17:45 and 47*

# DAY 3: THE GOD OF ALL COMFORT

***"Yea, though I walk through the valley of the shadow of death, I will fear no evil; for You are with me; Your rod and Your staff, they comfort me."***
***Psalm 23:4***

I was overwhelmed with sorrow for the lady who had brain cancer. I could imagine what she and her family were going through: the sorrow and uncertainty of life. Does God care?

My heart was broken for another lady who was suffering from stage three lymphatic cancer. The doctors recommended twelve rounds of chemotherapy. She did one but did not continue the rest. I understand her agony. The effect of chemo in the body is devastating. Who will like it? Who could help?

I praise the Father of compassion and the God of all comfort. His Word and promises are like a soothing balm in my aching body and bones. We could see His presence through the pages of His book, the Bible. We could feel His loving touch and comfort as we looked at Him through prayer and worship.

Isabel, my daughter, was already scheduled to fly to Australia to study at Hillsong College when we learned the devastating news about my sickness. I did not want the cancer to stop her from pursuing her dreams, so I encouraged her to go. She wrote: "God opened His arms and said "I am here," as I cried out to Him during Mama's first chemo treatment. God whispered His promise, "I will heal her," when I moved 15,544km away as she continued her battle. The Lord reminded me of His steadfast love and faithfulness as I fasted and prayed for her successful surgery. I continued to worship and worship and worship. Until her hair grew back, until her strength was renewed, and until she could hold up her hands in victory over her battle won, in Jesus' name. Then, after all is said and done, I will worship Him even more."

**Prayer:**

God, truly, You are our comfort. And with the comfort we received from You, we could minister and boldly tell those who are battling the "c" (cancer/covid) that the Big "C" (Christ) can help us and that the compassionate Christ is bigger than cancer or any difficult and painful circumstances. For those who are facing chemotherapy treatments, may they feel Your love as the chemo drugs enter their veins and quickly kill the cancer cells. Minimize the side effects and maximize the effectiveness of the chemo drugs. I pray they will receive the blessing and comfort from the God of all comfort. Thank You, Lord, our Menakhem!

***Menakhem - Hebrew name of the Messiah which means "comfort".***
***Read: Isaiah 40:1; Psalm 23:4; 71:21***

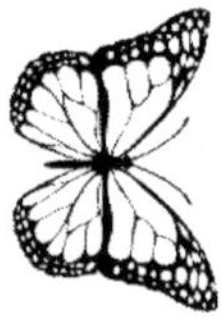

**Lord, I pray for comfort:**

________________________________________________

In Jesus Name. Amen.

*"In the multitude of my anxieties within me,*
*Your comforts delight my soul."*
*Psalm 94:19*

*"Blessed be the God and Father of our Lord Jesus Christ, the Father of mercies and the God of all comfort, who comforts us in all our tribulation, that we may be able to comfort those who are in any trouble, with the comfort with which we ourselves are comforted by God."*
*2 Corinthians 1:3-4*

# Day 4: The Lord who Sanctifies

***"I am the Lord who sanctifies you."***
***Exodus 31:13***

I was reminded of what God told Paul when he prayed for the thorn in his flesh, a messenger of Satan, to be taken away. The Amplified version of the Bible says it is "the gift of a handicap" that Satan's angel inflicted to torment, harass and get him down. He pleaded with God three times. He begged, but he received an unexpected answer. God promised that the weaker he gets, the stronger he becomes. He learned that if he drew himself in God's strength and power, he could overcome whatever situation he was in. God's grace is sufficient in ALL circumstances.

Mastectomy left an ugly scar on my body, a forever reminder of what I have gone through. But why would I be ashamed of this scar when it reminds me of how God has shown His power in me? I felt this was His way of sanctifying me. He set me apart through suffering so I would dedicate and depend my whole life to Him.

Tim, my eldest son, and his wife Nathasha gave me a watch with a note written on the Christmas card saying, "We hope that our gift to you would remind you of God's faithfulness during your trial and a standing testament of how God will continue to bring you through even in your darkest moments. Engraved on the back are three words: ***Strength.*** You have shown that no matter how weak you felt, you clung to the One that gives you strength. By God's grace, you slayed a Goliath from which few people return. ***Love.*** The amount of love that pours out from your heart is only a reflection of the relationship you have with our Heavenly Father. ***Courage.*** You looked Goliath in the eye, and despite all of your fears, you did not back down from the fight. You were strong and courageous because you had a God who had already claimed victory through His Son, Jesus. Let the watch symbolise the enemy's defeat and God's victory! Wear it proudly because our God is great!"

Truly, God's grace is abundant, even if I am missing some parts of my body. God's faithfulness is enough to make me complete when I am incomplete. God's love is all I needed to say: I am strong when I am weak!

**Prayer:**

Lord, thank You for Your abounding and sanctifying love. You alone make us whole, complete, and not lacking anything. May the scar on the body remind us to always trust in Your mercy and grace. May the thought of the pain that we have experienced be replaced with the memory of Your amazing power to heal. Lord God, may You strengthen the whole family as we all rely on Your mighty Spirit. May we find grace in Your eyes, Lord, and continue to sanctify us, YHWH Mekoddishkem!

***YHWH Mekoddishkem – Name of God meaning "The Lord who sanctifies you".***

***It is from the Hebrew word qadash, meaning set apart, consecrated, sanctified, prepared or dedicated.***
***Read: Exodus 33 and 34; Psalm 84:11***

**Lord, sanctify me:**

In Jesus Name, Amen!

***"The Lord is gracious and full of compassion, slow to anger and great in mercy." My strength is made perfect in weakness."***
***Psalm 145:8***

***"But none of these things move me; nor do I count my life dear to myself, so that I may finish my race with joy, and the ministry which I received from the Lord Jesus, to testify to the gospel of the grace of God."***
***Acts 20:24***

***"But He said to me, "My grace is sufficient for you, for My strength is made perfect in weakness."***
***2 Corinthians 12:9***

# DAY 5: THE GOD WHO HEARS AND LISTENS

***"Let my prayer be set before You as incense"***
***Psalm 141:2***

Prayer is the most powerful weapon we can have when dealing with any kind of sickness. When we humble ourselves to the God who hears, He will strengthen us to fight the battle. When we bow down to The Lord who listens, He will sustain us during this time of difficulty.

Prayer is like a sweet-smelling aroma that rises before the God of the Universe. It is a beautiful sound of music that rings to the ears of the Creator of heaven and earth. Taste and see that the Lord is good!

While cooking "bulalo" (a Filipino stew made from beef shanks and marrow bones), I started my devotion and prayer time. I prayed for blessings for my family, relatives, and friends. I ask God for healing for the sick, anointing to those who are serving God in the pulpit and salvation for those who do not know Christ personally as their Lord and Saviour.

After this time, I uttered, "Lord, may this prayer be set before You like an incense." In a concise while, I smelled burned food – the "bulalo" soup got burned! The smoke in the kitchen and the smell of the marrow bones filled the house like incense!

**Prayer:**

Lord, thank You for the opportunity to come to You in prayer. You give grace and mercy as we humble ourselves and believe You will answer our petitions and requests according to Your will. May You hear our prayers for those who are sick, those who struggle and feel invisible and forgotten by everyone else. You see even the deepest longings of our hearts. You always hear our groanings and answer our cries. Thank You, El Roi!

***El Roi - One of the names of God in the Hebrew Bible. Hagar called the Lord "You-Are-the-God-Who-Sees"; David called on YHWH Roi – "The Lord is my Shepherd". Read: Genesis 16:13-14; Psalm 23:1***

**Lord, hear my prayer:**

________________________________________________

________________________________________________

________________________________________________

________________________________________________

________________________________________________

________________________________________________

________________________________________________

In Jesus Name, Amen!

***"Now this is the confidence that we have in Him, that if we ask anything according to His will, He hears us." 1 John 5:14***

***"Ask, and it will be given to you; seek, and you will find; knock, and it will be opened to you." Matthew 7:7***

# Day 6: The Lord is There

***"The Lord is near to all who call upon Him…"***
***Psalm 145:18***

My journey with cancer has been long, hard, and depressing. But I am thankful for this experience because, just like Apostle Paul, God proved His faithfulness when I gave my total dependence on Him. His peace, protection, and presence were evident as I found my strength and joy in the Lord.

Apostle Paul said, "I face death everyday…" (See 1 Corinthians 15:31). He was hard pressed on every side, perplexed, persecuted, struck down, given over to death (See 2 Corinthians 4:8-12) and became the garbage of the world (See 1 Corinthians 4:13). He felt he received a death sentence and that this great pressure is far beyond his ability to endure, but he felt it was the best thing that could have happened to him because he was forced to trust God completely. God has proven His faithfulness to Paul. He also acknowledged the people who prayed for him and his ministry. For him, their prayers played a crucial part in the rescue operation (See 2 Corinthians 1:8-11). He praised the people's power through prayer!

I thank the Lord for He was with me during my journey with cancer. I acknowledge the many people who prayed for me. Some of them were from different parts of the world, and I have not met most of them yet. I want to tell you, "Praise

God for the answered prayers!" Thank you to ALL who became my prayer partners and prayer warriors.

**Prayer:**

Lord, thank You for hearing my cry and answering my prayer. Truly, You are the Sovereign God who is in control and knows every detail of our sufferings and agony. In those dark moments and confusing times, You are there. We are never alone. Make us aware of Your presence as You promised. Thank You for Your healing touch, my YHWH Shammah!

***YHWH Shammah - meaning "The Lord is there".***
***It refers to the fact that God Hears and He listens.***
***Read: Ezekiel 48:35***

**Lord, listen to my cry:**

In Jesus Name, Amen!

***"Fear not, for I have redeemed you;***
***I have called you by your name; You are Mine.***
***When you pass through the waters, I will be with you;***
***and through the rivers, they shall not overflow you.***
***When you walk through the fire, you shall not be burned,***
***nor shall the flame scorch you."***
***Isaiah 43:1-2***
***"I will never leave you nor forsake you."***
***Hebrews 13:5***

## Day 7: The Lord, Our Advocate

***"... we have an Advocate with the Father,***
***Jesus Christ the righteous."***
***1 John 2:1***

"How I long to be with you in this difficult time. The only thing I can do is to continually intercede for you and your family." This is the message of Susan, a Pastor's wife, my friend, and one of my prayer warriors. She obeyed God's instruction to pray for one another. She definitely followed Christ's example to intercede for God's people.

Susan prayed for me during my battle with cancer. The pandemic of loneliness due to covid-19 in 2020 made us even closer. Distance between the Philippines and Canada did not hinder us from communicating, thanks to the technology!

However, in September 2020, nine months after the covid started, she succumbed to illness, was hospitalized, and underwent hemoperfusion. Fifteen days after getting sick, at sixty years old, Susan went home to be with the Lord.

Prayer is important to know God's will in our life. It will help us to be wise on how to spend our remaining days, seeing that life is like a vapor that appears for a little time and then vanishes away. Prayer to the Almighty God will help us find strength, courage, and peace, especially when facing difficulties and hardships.

Jesus taught His disciples how to pray to the Father. Matthew 6:9-13 showed the A.C.T.S. (Adoration, Confession, Thanksgiving, Supplication) of worshipping the Father, the admonition to ask for the will of God, and the aim to follow the ways and acts of the Lord.

Pray your prayer; Jesus Christ is listening. He is also praying for you!

**Prayer:**

Lord, thank You for being our Advocate to the Father, always interceding for us. Thank You that You stand before the Father to plead our case. From the time we are formed in the womb to the time of our last breath, You are in control. While waiting for our appointed time, which is already written in Your Book of Life, help us be like You – always praying. Bring to mind those who are sick, lonely, and poor; those leaders in the government, church, business, and school; the doctors, nurses, teachers, missionaries, and pastors; those close to our heart, our family and friends, and those who are lost and need the Savior. Holy Spirit, come and lead us, renew and revive our prayer life in Jesus' Name.

**Paraclete – commonly refers to the Holy Spirit and is translated as 'advocate, 'counsellor' or 'helper.'**

Lord, come and lead me:

______________________________________________

______________________________________________

______________________________________________

______________________________________________

______________________________________________

______________________________________________

______________________________________________

In Jesus Name, Amen!

***"It is Christ who died, and furthermore is also risen, who is even at the right hand of God, who also makes intercession for us." Romans 8:34***

***"Lord, teach us to pray." Luke 11:1***

***"For there is one God and one Mediator between God and men, the Man Christ Jesus," 1 Timothy 2:5***

# DAY 8: THE LORD IS MY PROVIDER

***"And Abraham called the name of the place The-Lord-Will-Provide ..." Genesis 22:14***

**Greva Garcia Testimony**

In 2003, my husband and I lodged a visa application for Canada. Five years later, we were finally called in for our medical exam for permanent residency. Everything went well. But two months later, I went through a supposedly minor hysterectomy, only for the medical team to discover in the middle of the operation that I had ovarian cancer. Doctors were immediately called in to assist in taking out the visible tumors.

When I learned about my cancer, I thought of my kids, my husband, and, yes, my own death. I did not ask the Lord, "Why me?" or "Why so soon?" I managed to jump to the next question," What will happen to my family? Despite my fears, the Holy Spirit gave me a cheerful spirit. I turned my eyes to God and His love, Goodness, and Faithfulness. I told my husband, "Don't be scared; I have a bigger God than these tumors."

Sadly, after the surgery, I had to undergo six cycles of chemotherapy. This treatment is costly in the Philippines. I wondered, "Will we be able to pay and finish the six cycles?" God's answer was "yes." I completed my chemo, along with several tests. The funds did not come in all at once but in stages at just the right time. It taught us to trust God's ways and timing. He moved the hearts of so many people who contributed to my hospital expenses. God not only provided for my treatment, but He also spared me from more serious side effects of chemotherapy. He protected my lungs and my liver, although I lost my hair two weeks after my first cycle. The treatment was completed.

God moved in ways beyond my expectations and imagination. He has proven His faithfulness. He never left us in times of need. As a result, my husband gave his life to God. He is my YHWH Yireh – the God who provides!

**Prayer:**

Lord, thank you that You are Omniscient – the All-knowing God who provides for all our physical, emotional, and spiritual needs. You give even before we ask. You shower us with Your blessings even if we do not deserve them. You complete us even when we do not give our total love and devotion to You. That is how You loved us. That is who You are.

***YHWH Yireh- The Lord Will Provide***
***Read: Genesis 22:13-14***

**Lord, thank You for Your provision:**

In Jesus Name, Amen!

***"Therefore, I say to you, do not worry about life, what you will eat or what you will drink; nor about your body, what you will put on. Is not life more than food and the body more than clothing? Look at the birds of the air, for they neither sow nor reap nor gather into barns; yet your heavenly Father feeds them.***

***Are you not one of more value than they?"***
***Matthew 6:25-26***

***"And my God shall supply all your need according to His riches in glory by Christ Jesus."***
***Philippians 4:19***

# Day 9: The Lord is My Rock

***"The Lord is my rock and my fortress and my deliverer;
My God, my strength, in whom I will trust…"
Psalm 18:2***

**Greva Garcia Testimony (cont.)**

In 2009, we finally immigrated to Canada with hopes for a new start and a new life. Not long after, I received news that my mother was diagnosed with terminal cancer and was dying. Flying back to the Philippines, I got the news that she had already passed away. The good news, however, was that my mother was in God's loving and tender hand, free from pain. God's faithfulness during my first battle with cancer has been an instrument in moving her to fully place her faith in Jesus Christ.

Back from that trip, I was once again met by new test results that showed a recurrence of ovarian cancer. Strangely, a growing feeling of excitement with the Lord in this battle occurred again. On this "one-on-one" with the Lord, I realized that no one could fully comprehend my pain except the Lord, who created me and knows me well. I have to face my giants again. But I know no giants are too big if God is my God. Psalm 73:26 says, "My flesh and heart may fail, but God is the strength of my heart and my portion forever."

God is victorious over death, strengthens the weak, brings healing, and comforts the weary. I am one of many recipients of His grace. God answers prayers. It can move mountains, and nothing is impossible with Him.

God's promises are a source of joy and the foundations of true courage. Our victory is secure. How could we not be courageous?

It is difficult, but I have learned to leave all my worries in His hands. God has reminded me of the "great things" He has done in the past and who He is in the present. I know I wouldn't have grown in faith in Him had He not let me go through these trials.

It was not until I walked with Him through some profound troubles in life that I discovered He could lead me to find refreshment in Him right amid my difficulties. We're all living on borrowed time, and by His grace, I am now living purposefully on this borrowed time for Him. Only as one who has walked with Him through such dark valleys can I console, comfort, or encourage others in similar situations. The simple fact is that water can only flow in a ditch, channel, or valley- so in my life, the love of God can flow only through the valleys carved and cut by excruciating experiences.

I hope and pray that my testimony will encourage you through Christ Jesus, our Lord. To God be the glory!

**Prayer:**

Lord, like David, who slayed Goliath, You will strengthen us to fight our own giant. This is also Your battle, which You already won when You died on the cross and rose from the dead. With Your stripes, we are healed. Your resurrection gives us hope. Thank You that in solid rock, we stand. You are the Solid Rock, the Strong Tower, and the Rock of Ages. Thank You for being our YHWH Tsuri!

***YHWH Tsuri- The Lord Is My Rock***
***Read: Psalm 18:2; 2 Samuel 22:2 and 47***

**Lord, thank You that You are my Rock:**

_______________________________________________

_______________________________________________

_______________________________________________

_______________________________________________

_______________________________________________

_______________________________________________

_______________________________________________

In Jesus Name, Amen!

***"He only is my rock and my salvation,
He is my defense; I shall not be greatly moved."
Psalm 62:2***

***"The Lord lives! Blessed be my Rock!
Let the God of my salvation be exalted."
Psalm 18:46***

***"No one is holy like the Lord, For there is none besides You, Nor is there any rock like our God."
1 Samuel 2:2***

# Day 10: The Lord is My Potter

***"But now, O Lord, You are our Father; We are the clay, and You our potter; and all we are the work of Your hand." Isaiah 64:8***

"I never heard her complain until the very end," said Tessie, Belle's sister, when my friend passed away.

In 2019, after Belle's cancer metastasized to her lungs, she went back home to the Philippines to be with her family while doing her treatments.

We exchanged notes on how to win the war with "c." We prayed for each other. She agreed that this was the Lord's battle. She fully trusted God as her Healer. She remembered telling God the first time she had it that she would be His "project" that would give a living testimony of His goodness. She believed that God is our Potter and we are His clay. And that the Potter will mold the clay to create a beautiful masterpiece that could give honor and glory to Him.

Belle wrote to me once: "Being with Christ does not mean to have everyday happiness. Of course, there are loads to carry. But trials and problems come your way; consider it a complete joy. They are God's blessings which bring steadfastness, and as a good soldier of Christ, you have to face the hardships with courage from God, who strengthens you."

Belle did not give up. She fought hard until the year 2022, when she breathed her last.

**Prayer:**

Lord, thank You for placing us in good hands. You are Sovereign and never make mistakes. The pressure when You mold us and shape us can be difficult and frustrating. But we trust and commit our lives in Your loving hands. Mold us into the kind of person You want us to be, Your masterpiece that will bring glory to Your Name. We trust You, our Yatsar!

***Yatsar- Hebrew name for God meaning***
***"The Lord Is My Potter"***
***Read: Isaiah 64; Jeremiah 18***

**Lord, thank You for being my Potter:**

____________________________________________
____________________________________________
____________________________________________
____________________________________________
____________________________________________
____________________________________________
____________________________________________

In Jesus Name, Amen!

***"... can I not do with you as this potter? Says the Lord.***
***"Look, as the clay is in the potter's hand,***
***so you are in My hand…"***
***Jeremiah 18:6***

***"For I consider that the sufferings of this present time are not worthy to be compared with the glory which shall be revealed in us."***
***Romans 8:18***

## Day 11: The Lord is my Stronghold

***"The name of the Lord* is *a strong tower;***
***The righteous run to it and are safe."***
***Proverbs 18:10***

**Myrna Roman Testimony**

I'M A SURVIVOR! And I thank God for my second life, for waking me up after a deep sleep.

It was February 18, 2011. I was busier than usual preparing for three events- two in Mindanao and one in Tagaytay. I took a break to have lunch with my colleagues at the nearby food court when I felt a sharp and intense headache - the worst pain I had ever had. The headache was so severe, like a lightning bolt had hit my head.

My last memory of that incident was hearing my colleagues calling out my name before I passed out. I was brought for first aid at the Shangrila clinic before being rushed to the Medical City in Ortigas, Pasig City. The doctors said I had to be operated on right away. They were racing against time.

I had a ruptured aneurysm on the left side of my brain. An operation was done to save my life. The doctors performed a procedure called surgical clipping. God held me during the long hours of surgery. After 7 hours, I woke up and opened my eyes. The doctor called me a miracle patient. Three days after the surgery, I recuperated. I did not lose my memory or my physical strength. I was so blessed to have a new life.

The doctor said it would take at least six months to even years to completely recover and restore normal everyday functions. Three months after the operation, my doctor was surprised to see that I had fully recovered. He gave me a clean bill of health. It's a miracle!

I find brain aneurysms almost unique. I could not understand the dramatic event and have been asking many whys and hows. At the same time, I was very thankful and happy to see my family and friends who stayed by my side. The doctors, nurses, and hospital staff were also very supportive and kind. I felt their love and concern for me. I am grateful for people's extended help and financial assistance covering my hospital bills.

That was after my near-death experience. I am one of the blessed few who survived a ruptured brain aneurysm. It was a tough fight and a unique battle- but I won!

I am very thankful to God for my second life. Truly, He empowers us to live in victory and overcome all the troubles in our lives. As Matthew 19:26 says, "With God, all things are possible."

**Prayer:**

Lord, You are a miracle worker. You covered us with the blood of the Lamb from head to toe. The same power that raised Jesus from death will be the same power that will crush the sickness in our bodies. You healed the blind, the lame, and even the dead, like Lazarus. You have shown Your divine power by healing the sick and the dying like me. Nothing is too hard for You. You are my strong tower; we do not have to be afraid. We can run to You for refuge. We can safely lean on Your promises. You are my Migdal-Oz!

***Migdal-Oz – Hebrew name for God, meaning my strong tower or stronghold***
***Read: Proverbs 18***

**Lord, You are our strong tower and refuge:**

In Jesus Name, Amen!

***"Oh, give thanks to the God of heaven!***
***For His mercy endures forever."***
***Psalm 136:26***

***"For You have been a shelter for me,***
***A strong tower from the enemy."***
***Psalm 61:3***

# Day 12: The Lord, Our Warrior

***"Yet in all these things we are more than conquerors through Him who loved us."***
***Romans 8:37***

**Ritche O. Olivares Testimony**

In 2022, I was faced with a challenge. I suffered severe pain in my right abdomen. On June 21, I was diagnosed with incarcerated indirect inguinal hernia on the right abdomen, a rare case for women. So, I underwent a hernioplasty and excision of lipoma by cutting off the ligament. The procedure was successful, and I returned to work after three days (June 27, but still recuperating).

On August 24 that year, I experienced hallucinations for the very first time. It was a pleasant, enjoyable, and beautiful kind of experience. I saw no sadness, sorrow, hunger, or pain. My mouth kept declaring, "Continue to preach the gospel. Don't be ashamed to share His Word... Brethren, Heaven is real," to some of my fellow workers from different regions of the Philippines. It was the 2nd day of the annual planning in Zamboanga, Mindanao. I thanked God that He did not allow me to faint or to become comatose.

In the evening, I prayed to our Almighty Sovereign God to show mercy to me. I thank my friend Remy, head of a child care development center based in Bacolod, who stayed to pray and sing with me. Also, my other friend, Stenili, our Child Development Program (CDP) Coordinator of AMG Philippines, gave her full support for me.

On August 26, I travelled to Davao to visit my brother Romar and his family. There, I met his friend, an oncologist. He prayed and recommended me to a nephrologist upon seeing the result of my creatinine level of 6.3. On August 29, the nephrologist declared that I have a stage 5 chronic kidney disease with a critical hemoglobin level. I was recommended for dialysis. I was hesitant to undergo dialysis, but after further explanations and with the support of my siblings, I became fully determined. I believed it was God's way of extending my life and to continue serving Him.

From August 31 to September 7, I underwent surgery for internal jugular vein catheter insertion on the right chest in a medical center in South Cotabato. I was unconscious for five days. Many prayed for me, my family, relatives, colleagues, Christian brethren, and friends in Luzon, Visayas, Mindanao, Canada, Germany, and the USA.

Praise God! On the 7th day, I was back to being conscious. However, I was advised to have dialysis twice a week. At first, I felt discouraged and hopeless. But I remember Paul's example and realize we must trust God in every situation. We need to depend on Him. God provided everything he needed. That caused my eagerness to grow more and share the gospel with people. I encourage them to have an intimate relationship with our Lord Jesus as their personal Lord and Savior.

On September 10, I returned home to Bacolod, where Katrina accompanied me. I thank God that I surrounded myself with people who cared for, loved, prayed for, and looked out for me always and made my life meaningful. I'm so grateful; He has given me family, friends, and fellow workers who bless me daily with kind words and actions. I thank God for the strength He gives me daily and for everything in my life. Good and bad. They were blessings and lessons in life. I'm so grateful for them all.

By God's grace, I have learned to be more grateful to Him for all the pressures and hardships I encounter every day. Praise God through my illness I have become more than a conqueror!

**Prayer:**

Lord, You are the King of all heaven and earth Who goes before us. You already conquered our enemy even before we fought our battle. With Your power, we can be more than conquerors like You! With Your stripes, we are healed. Nothing is impossible for You. You give wisdom to those who seek You. You reveal Yourself to those who trust in You. Help us to remember that You are our YHWH Tsaba!

***Tsaba - Hebrew name of God that means***
***"The Lord our warrior"***
***Read: 1 Samuel 17:38-51 and Romans 8***

**Lord, I believe I could conquer this trial:**

__________________________________________________________________

In Jesus Name, Amen!

*"And He said to me, "My grace is sufficient for you, for My strength is made perfect in weakness." Therefore, most gladly I will rather boast in my infirmities, that the power of Christ may rest upon me."*
*2 Corinthians 12:9*

*"The Lord will fight for you,*
*And you shall hold your peace."*
*Exodus 14:14*

*"You are of God, little children, and have overcome them, because He who is in you is greater than he who is in the world."*
*1 John 4:4*

# Day 13: The Author of Life

***"...the Prince of life, whom God raised from the dead..."* *Acts 3:15***

Jing, my friend, received the devastating news. She has a few months to live. After a year of remission from colon cancer, the cancer metastasized to other parts of the body. I, too, was devastated. She was cleared of cancer when I started my own journey of it. When I got healed, hers came back with a vengeance. Part of the letter I wrote to her says:

"Since no one knows the future, who can tell someone else what is to come?... no one has power over the time of death." (Ecclesiastes 8:7-8). No one – not even the most brilliant doctor in the world knows when the hour of death will come.

However, death is the destiny of everyone, and the day of death is better than the day of birth. As everyone comes naked from the mother's womb, so they depart (See Ecclesiastes 5:15; 7:1-2). God turns people back to dust. He sweeps people away in the sleep of death, like the grass - it springs up in the morning, but by evening, it dries and withers (See Psalm 90:3-6). I know it will be tough, but God is a faithful and compassionate God. He will never leave you nor forsake you (See Hebrews 13:5).

Jing lived for a few more years before her appointed time to meet the Lord came.

**Prayer:**

Lord, help us who are confronted with death to take courage. Help us to fight the good fight of faith, finish the race, and complete the task You have given with joy in our hearts. We know You will be there every step of the way – in every pain, every tear, when we are afraid, and when we cannot understand Your will. You have complete control of our entire life, from beginning to end. You alone are the Author of our life- Yeshua, The Messiah!

***JESUS - The Author of Life***
***YESHUA - in Hebrew is a verbal derivative from***
***"to rescue", "to deliver"***
***Read: Acts 3:13-15; Proverbs 8; 30:4; John 1:1; 3:13***

**Lord, thank You for my life:**

______________________________
______________________________
______________________________
______________________________
______________________________
______________________________
______________________________

In Jesus Name, Amen!

*"We are confident, yes, well pleased rather to be absent from the body and to be present with the Lord."*
*2 Corinthians.5:8*

*"In the beginning was the Word, and the Word was with God, and the Word was God.*
*He was in the beginning with God.*
*All things were made through Him, and without Him nothing was made that was made.*
*In Him was life, and the life was the light of men."*
*John 1:1-4*

*"He who has the Son has life;*
*he who does not have the Son of God does not have life."*
*1 John 5:12*

# Day 14: The Lord is My Healer

***"I am the Lord who heals you."***
***Exodus 15:26b***

**Milagros Palad Gonzales Testimony**

I am Mila. In September 2004, I woke up with blood in my blanket. My husband took me to the nearest hospital. I had an ultrasound, and the result showed the blood came from the polyps inside my cervix. I had minor surgery and had some tissue taken for biopsy. After a long wait, the result was given - it was stage three cervical cancer.

The next treatment was a unique and expensive procedure called "brachytherapy," followed by 26 days of "cobalt" or "radiation." Then another surgery for a hysterectomy was done.

Since then, every morning, I thank God for healing me. I praise Him for the new life and new beginning that He has given me. My Redeemer and Master proved to me that His Word is true when He said:

***"I will never leave you nor forsake you."***
***So we may boldly say: "The Lord is my helper, I will not fear, what can man do to me?" Hebrews 13:5-6***

I am seventy-nine years old and still rejoicing for what God has done to me. It is always my joy to tell people that God loves us so much and that He is our Healer. He is our YHWH Rapha.

**Prayer:**

Lord, thank You for the gift of life and health. You are the Great Physician who could heal cancer and all kinds of sickness. Let us feel Your presence in our time of pain, doubt, and fear. Strengthen our weaknesses and help us have complete confidence in Your loving care. You can heal us and allow us to see Your goodness in the land of the living. Truly, You are our YHWH Rapha!

***YHWH Rhapa- The Lord Who Heals***
***Read: Exodus 15:26***

**Lord, heal me…**

____________________________________________
____________________________________________
____________________________________________
____________________________________________
____________________________________________
____________________________________________
____________________________________________

In Jesus Name, Amen!

***"For You have delivered my soul from death.***
***My eyes from tears, and my feet from falling.***
***I will walk before the Lord in the land of the living."***
***Psalm 116:8-9***

***"Heal me, O Lord, and I shall be healed;***
***Save me, and I shall be saved,***
***For You*** are ***my praise."***
***"For I will restore health to you***
***And heal you of your wounds,' says the Lord…"***
***Jeremiah 17:14 and 30:17***

# DAY 15: THE LORD IS MY PROTECTOR

***"He who dwells in the secret place of the Most High shall abide under the shadow of the Almighty. I will say of the Lord, "He is my refuge and my fortress; My God, in Him I will trust"***
***Psalm 91:1-2***

The beginning of Psalm 91 spoke of the names of God: Most High- Elyon; Almighty- Shadday; The Lord- YHWH; and My God- Elohay/ Elohim. He is described as our shelter, shadow, refuge, fortress, shield, buckler, dwelling place, deliverer, rescuer, and protector- our Salvation!

Psalm 91 gives comfort in God in facing the battle with cancer and, most recently, the fear of coronavirus. It reminds us of the infinite God that is fiercer than these small "c's" of life!

## The "Big C" Conquered My Small "c"

### Susana Fadul Roco Testimony

My best friend said, "I have a verse for you! Read it daily and claim it! We need this, especially now." I had it printed in big letters, placed in transparent protective covering, and posted at eye-level, above the bathroom light switch so I may read and declare daily: **Psalm 91**

One day, an unexpected call came from my Primary Doctor, "Don't be alarmed. I suspect you have cancer of the pancreas." At first, I was not alarmed as my mind went, 'Do research. You can beat this one!' But as I researched, my hopes got dimmer. Pancreatic cancer is an invasive c that has no known cure. An Aunt recently passed away within a couple of months after diagnosis. A famous advanced thinker also succumbed to pancreatic c. With my symptoms getting vivid, I knew I had the c. I got worried sick. Worse, I couldn't get an appointment to see an Oncologist because of the long waitlist. If I wait, I'll be gone before the end of the year! I could not and should not wait. I was deteriorating, so, as advised by a concerned Aunt, a retired Nurse Manager, I requested to be referred to another Specialist outside the system.

So, I was scheduled for an abdominal CT scan and had a Tele-consultation with a Specialist. I fasted for 12 hours, but upon registration, I was told my name was not on the list! I tried to reason with the medical staff but to no avail. I had to reschedule. No walk-ins! I went home hungry, angry, and frustrated! A debilitating migraine was starting. I had to calm down, so I went to my cool Private Room, switched on the light, and slunk in the covered seat with a deep sigh. "Dear God, please help!" Then, the verse above the light switch called out to me!

Psalm 91! I read it, reread it, and declared it out loud. Then I prayed, "Dear God, why was I so blind? You have given me my Salvation through the Big C, Christ! Dear Father Almighty, I claim Your protection now! And thank You for letting me know You." Soon, I got a call for the CT Scan appointment. On the same day, the Oncologist called me to assure me that the suspected CA was benign. A repeat MRI every two years is recommended to monitor any changes. I was so thankful. Deep within, I acknowledge that the Big C, Christ, conquered the small c of Susana!

**Prayer:**

Lord, thank You for being our Protector, the One Who hides us under the shadow of His wings. You fight for us every step of the way with Your goodness and mercy. You surround us with Your love and faithfulness. Because You watch over us, we will be safe and protected from any harm. You are our Elohim Shomri!

***Elohim Shomri-***
***The Hebrew translation for God is My Protector***
***Read: Psalm 91, 20, 61, 121***

**Lord, thank You for Your protection:**

In Jesus Name, Amen!

***"Because you have made the Lord, who is my refuge, even the Most High, your dwelling place, no evil shall befall you, nor shall any plague come near your dwelling; for He shall give His angels charge over you…"***
***Psalm 91:9-11***

***"He shall call upon Me, and I will answer him; I will be with him in trouble; I will deliver him and honor him. With long life I will satisfy him, and show him My salvation."***
***Psalm 91: 15-16***

# DAY 16: THE LORD, OUR HELPER

***"Come to Me, all you who labor and are heavy laden, and I will give you rest. Take My yoke upon you and learn from me, for I am gentle and lowly in heart, and you will find rest for your souls. For My yoke is easy and My burden is light."***
***Matthew 11:28-30***

Caregivers are blessings from God.

They show compassion (desire to alleviate the suffering of the one they love), understanding (patience when the sick person becomes irritable and hard to deal with because of the pain), long-suffering (willing to experience sleep deprivation or give up his or her own career and aspirations in life), faith (believing for a favorable or positive outcome of the situation), and confidence (that with God's love and strength, he or she will be able to be God's hands and feet in helping others). The Scripture talks about taking care of loved ones. It says: ***"Whoever does not care for his own relatives, especially his own family members, has turned against the faith and is worse than someone who does not believe in God." (1 Timothy 5:8).***

**Prayer:**

Father God, listen to the prayers of the caregivers. Grant them strength, patience, and understanding as they care for the sick and the dying. May they be Your hands and feet in showing Your tender touch and care. With God's love as motivation, they will be a blessing to those who are suffering. Let them know that their selfless devotion and love are greatly appreciated. Above all, You are the loving God who helps us – our Yehovah Ezer!

***Yehovah Ezer – Hebrew translation of "LORD; He is our help"***

***"Assuredly, I say to you, in as much as you did* it *to one of the least of these My brethren, you did* it *to Me." Matthew 25:40***

***"The LORD is my strength and my shield;***
***My heart trusted in Him, and I am helped;***
***Therefore my heart greatly rejoices,***
***And with my song I will praise Him."***
***Psalm 28:7***

## God's Love Energizes

### Edith Arabe Fadul Testimony

***Unwell Loved Ones:*** Achievers and active; bright and brilliant. These were my parents, Martin and Nina. But eventually, both became bedridden and dependent on 24/7 caregiving. I loved our conversations, but eventually, I could only look into their eyes to talk with them while reassuringly holding their hands.

My heart was breaking when Mom, a prolific writer, struggled to hold up a pen due to a major bleed stroke in 2013. (After her 1st stroke in 2005, she persevered to write using her left hand.) We gently distracted her to other goals. Henceforth, she gladly dictated the poetry ringing in her mind, immortalized in photo books. Mom was initially taking in nutrition via a nasal-gastric tube. But we persisted in feeding her pureed food for 5 months until her throat strengthened, and she ate by mouth. Despite her physical pain and emotional load, Mom demonstrated wit and humor with her family, therapists, and caregivers. Mom sang with Papa at times, though she labored with the words. Mom joined her Savior in October 2018, blessed with 91 well-lived years.

Papa became blind with a cataract at 87 years old. This is really sad for a voracious reader. His 24/7 care started in 2018 after a mild stroke; he had Parkinson's disease and prostate concerns. Papa got well in 2019. Papa and I would have long chats on life, management principles, and abstract concepts. He loved the details of my 2019 Pilgrimage trip to Israel. But in 2021, his words became few. He could no longer count backwards or in Spanish in his morning exercises. Papa healed from severe pneumonia in 2021 but occasionally needed oxygen support. Papa joined his Lord in January 2023, blessed with 95 full years.

***Caregiving Daughter.*** As a caregiving daughter, I felt my parents' pain. I always prayed for their comfort. I read up on their maladies, constantly consulted our Cardio-Internist family doctor and other doctors, and explored naturopathic approaches. I tasted what they would eat and mimicked how they moved for my better understanding. I made time for their care.

God provided well for us by making professional caregivers, therapists, expert medical teams, tests, medicines, supplements, and nutritious food available. At hospitals and drugstores, my heart goes to those who are in pain due to their bills. At the supermarket, I get frustrated not finding healthier options.

Caregiving can be physically, mentally, emotionally, and spiritually exhausting. God enabled me to be on top of the situation, harmonize the different factors, and have timely information for appropriate action. He gave me rest after I had to take 12- to 16-hour care shifts when no one else was available.

***God's Love Never Fails.*** God has miraculously healed my parents and gave them long, fruitful years. As a caregiving daughter, I drew strength and joy from the Word of God daily. I asked for wisdom on the decisions to be made. I asked for patience, kindness, and perseverance. He enabled me to pour from an overflowing cup and was conscious of self-care and a healthy lifestyle. I know that there are times I could have done better. But I have been assured that they have forgiven me. As God has forgiven me, I have forgiven myself and shared with others God's bountiful providence, His love that never fails.

***"Love suffers long and is kind…love … bears all things, believes all things, hopes all things, endures all things. Love never fails".***
***I Corinthians 13: 4 – 8***

**Lord, thank You for being our helper. I pray for caregivers as a channel of Your help. And I pray for:**

_______________________________________________

_______________________________________________

_______________________________________________

_______________________________________________

_______________________________________________

_______________________________________________

_______________________________________________

In Jesus Name, Amen!

***"For God is not unjust to forget your work and labor of love which you have shown toward His name, in that you have ministered to the saints, and do minister."***
***Hebrews 6:10***

# DAY 17: THE AUTHOR AND FINISHER OF OUR FAITH

***"…let us run with endurance the race that is set before us, looking unto Jesus, the author and finisher of our faith, who for the joy that was set before Him endured the cross, despising the shame, and has sat down at the right hand of the throne of God."***
***Hebrews 12:2***

**Milagros Cham Nava Testimony**

This love story focuses on some of my conversations with God and His miracles.

In April 2022, I was diagnosed with multiple myeloma stage 2, blood cancer of the plasma cells, which is said to be incurable. I underwent chemotherapy and a stem cell transplant to extend my life.

I questioned God when I got the diagnosis. He reminded me that He is my loving King who died for me even when I was still a sinner (Romans 5:8). I repented and asked for forgiveness.

I bargained with the Lord, "I know heaven is a wonderful place, but I want to grow old with my kids." God responded with the story of the raising of Lazarus, saying that this sickness will not end in death, but its purpose is to glorify God (John11:4). And I will see the glory of God if I believed (John11:40). He also reminded me that He gave Hezekiah15 more years to live when he asked (2Kings 20:5-6). I will be a living testimony of His glory. He reminded me of my purpose to worship Him and bring people to His Kingdom.

Silly, but I also doubted if I were going to Heaven. God said that since I believed in Jesus, Heaven is my home (Ephesians 2:8-9). He also further asked me, "Whose voice do you hear?" and I said, "Yours, Lord." I had peace after. I dreamt after that, death came for me, and I felt this terror in my heart, thinking of spending eternity in hell. I asked the Lord about this, to which He replied, "so that you will know the terror in the hearts of unbelievers when they die. So that My children will have the urgency and courage to tell others about Me."

God was not surprised with this cancer. He told me He's got me. At the onset, my church sent me flowers with a card saying God's got you. A friend shared her vision of me with Jesus sitting beside me, kissing my temple, and saying, "I've got your back." Another friend gave a devotional entitled "You've got this because God's got you."

During the first month, I was screaming in pain. I became an invalid in a wheelchair. I had hematoma whenever I was pricked with a needle, which was often. I was restless all night. One night, my daughter had God's wisdom regarding my sleeping position and directed me to it. I had my first good, miraculous sleep that night. I even dreamed of people called Ancients surrounding me and repeatedly saying, "Why don't they know this? We all know this. They should know this. If they don't, they should ask." The Lord told me to ask Him because He knows all the answers. When I woke up, the swollen, tender hematomas on both my hands were miraculously gone. That's God and His miracles!

I started this cancer journey focusing on the sickness instead of on Jesus. When I asked God how He wanted to move forward, He told me to remember the miracles in my life. When I did that, He addressed every fear I had.

There is no formula for our relationship with God. All we need to be is to be clingy, listen to Him closely, trust fully, and obey recklessly. God promised me in Jeremiah 30:17, "As for you, Mila, I'll come with healing, curing the incurable."

**Prayer:**

Thank You, Jesus, for being the Author and Finisher of our faith. You said, "Believe," and if it is according to Your will, You will show us Your power, and we will experience miracles in our lives. Lord, help my unbelief. Remove negative feelings of doubt, fear, grumbling, and complaining and replace them with faith, courage, hope, and peace that we can only find in You, our Lord and Savior.

***Jesus – Author and Finisher of Faith***
***Read: Hebrews 11 & 12***

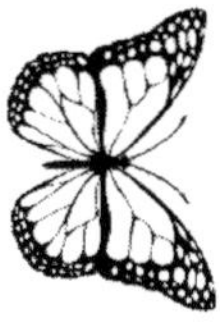

**Lord, I believe that You will complete what You have started:**

_______________________________________________

_______________________________________________

_______________________________________________

_______________________________________________

_______________________________________________

_______________________________________________

_______________________________________________

In Jesus Name, Amen!

***"Lord, I believe, help my unbelief!"***
***Mark 9:24***

***"Now faith is the substance of things hoped for, the evidence of things not seen."***
***Hebrews 11:1***

***"My brethren, count it all joy when you fall into various trials, knowing that the testing of your faith produces patience… let him ask in faith, with no doubting, for he who doubts is like a wave of the sea driven and tossed by the wind…"***
***James 1:2-8***

# DAY 18: THE LORD IS MY STRENGTH

***"For I consider that the sufferings of this present time are not worthy to be compared with the glory which shall be revealed in us."***
***Romans 8:18***

The splash of the water at Vero Beach, Florida, was so refreshing that we could not help but continue walking on the beach farther away from the shore. But when the big wave came, Elaine, Aileen, and I tumbled. We could not stand up. The waves continued to pull us into the deep! God provided a Good Samaritan to help us stand and return to shore. We had a good laugh. It was fun and a happy memory!

In September 2018, my daughter Angela, my friend Aileen, and I visited our family friend Elaine Jackson in Florida, USA. She was my daughter's Godmother. It has been a long time since we have not seen her. Elaine became our tour guide, driving us around despite suffering from a hip problem, which made it very difficult for her to move and walk. We went to Disney World, the beach, and other places. I brought our old pictures and videos to reminisce about the past. She was so happy to see them and watch the 'good old times' videos.

She laughed when she saw the picture of the newborn baby Angela. She recalled what happened in the delivery room. She did not have children of her own, so it was fascinating for her to be there with my husband. After I gave birth, the doctor handed the baby to my husband, and then he quickly 'turned over' the baby to her.

Our friendship began when we immigrated to Canada in 1994. Pastor Marvin Jackson was our first Pastor here. They have been outstanding and helpful to my family, like parents to us. That's why when I gave birth to Angela, we asked them to be her Godparents.

Pastor Jackson was a US war veteran, became a Pastor, and was called to lead a church in Canada. After a year, he and his wife moved back to the USA. He became a Pastor in another church and eventually led the ABA Disaster Relief Ministries in Florida. In the year 2015, Pastor Jackson suffered and died of cancer.

In the year 2018, after more than two decades of not seeing Elaine, we decided to visit her. It was after my cancer treatments. The visit was a happy and memorable reunion. We encourage her to stay strong so she can attend the wedding of Angela in the future.

At the beginning of 2019, she had a hip replacement and had to stay in a nursing home to recuperate. However, she had a heart attack and then later on was found to have cancer. She was always in good spirits every time I sent her messages. She knows that she is not alone in her battle. As God promised, He will never ever leave her nor forsake her.

Looking forward to that joyous occasion when she meets her Savior face to face and sees the love of her life again, her husband, Elaine, sings her favorite song at church for the last time. The Hymn was titled "In the Garden," and the lyrics of the chorus go like this:

"And He walks with me, and He talks with me,
And He tells me I am His own
And the joy we share as we tarry there,
None other has ever known."

February 2021, she bid goodbye to her earthly body and was welcomed into the Heavenly Kingdom of her Lord and Savior, Jesus Christ!

**<u>Prayer:</u>**

Lord, thank You that in solid rock we stand. You are the Solid Rock, the Strong Tower, and the Rock of Ages. We will hide in the shadow of the Mighty and Faithful God. You are trustworthy, perfect in all Your ways. In You, we are secured and will never be shaken. You are our El Sali!

***El Sali – The Lord is my Strength or the Lord is my Rock***
***Read: Psalm 18***

**Lord, You are my Rock:**

______________________________________________
______________________________________________
______________________________________________
______________________________________________
______________________________________________
______________________________________________
______________________________________________

In Jesus Name, Amen!

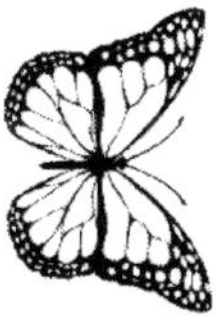

*"Blessed* be *the Lord my Rock,*
*Who trains my hands for war,* and *my fingers for battle.*
*My lovingkindness and my fortress, my high tower*
*and my deliverer, My shield and the One*
*in whom I take refuge…"*
*Psalm 144:1-2*

*"From the end of the earth I will cry to You,*
*When my heart is overwhelmed;*
*Lead me to the rock that is higher than I."*
*Psalm 61:2*

# DAY 19: JESUS - THE ONLY WAY

***"Jesus said to him "I am the way, the truth, and the life. No one comes to the Father except through Me."***
***John 14:6***

"Goodbye to my Mama… the arms that held me for so many years, the beautiful voices no longer I hear, she's in Jesus' arms, and He's talking to her…Thank you, Mama…" This was the song from the movie Prairie Home Companion. It echoed in my ears as I looked at the clouds outside the airplane returning to Canada. I attended the burial of my Mother in the Philippines.

I was happy for her. At age 77, Auring, as her friends call her, has gone to be with the Lord.

Looking back, when I took care of her in the hospital, she was so desperate to end her life. She was asking for mercy killing. I wouldn't say I liked her look when she entered the dialysis room. She wanted to scream and say she had enough. But no voice would come out because of the tubes of the mechanical ventilator in her mouth. I told her God knows her sufferings, and He loves her and cares for her. Yes, I was guilty. I prayed to God to just take her life instead of seeing her suffer.

October 1, 2006, is when she entered that dark door of death that signaled the last chapter of her life on earth. Into the loving arms of her Creator, she was ushered to the first chapter of her life in eternity. Now she understands that all those sufferings were not worthy to be compared with the glory of God that was revealed in her.

**Prayer:**

Father, thank You for the free gift of salvation You gave to us through Jesus Christ, Your only begotten Son. Your Word clearly says that You alone is the Way, the Truth, and the Life. We are assured of eternal life as we believe in You and what You have done on the cross. Because of Your ultimate sacrifice as the "Lamb of God," You saved us from our sins through faith. Because You rose from the dead, we can look forward to a grand reunion in heaven with our departed loved ones who trusted in You. You are our El khayyai!

***El khayyai – God of my life in the Hebrew text of Psalm 42:8. He is the source of life. Read: Deuteronomy 32:39; Job 12:10***

**Lord Jesus, I believe that You are the only Way:**

In Jesus Name, Amen!

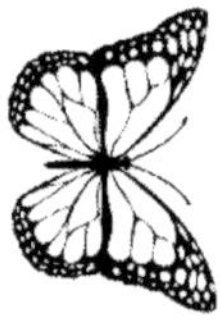

*"And God will wipe away every tear from their eyes; there shall be no more death, nor sorrow, nor crying… no more pain…"*
*Revelation 21:4*

*"Let not your heart be troubled; you believe in God, believe also in Me. In My Father's house are many mansions…*
*I go to prepare a place for you…*
*I will come again and receive you to Myself;*
*that where I am,* there *you may be also."*
*John 14:1-3*

*"Let it be known to you all, and to all the people of Israel, that by the name of Jesus Christ of Nazareth, whom you crucified, whom God raised from the dead, by Him this man stands here before you whole. This is the 'stone which was rejected by you builders, which has become the chief cornerstone.' Nor is there salvation in any other, for there is no other name under heaven given among men by which we must be saved."*
*Acts 4:10-12*

***"And now abide***
***FAITH, HOPE, LOVE***
***These three; the greatest of these is LOVE."***
***1 Corinthians 13:13***

*(The following narrative talks about faith, hope, and love. It is about the struggles and triumphs of my friend Wilma, who, in two and a half years, fought the good fight of faith. It is about the sacrifices and hope of her husband, Perry, who became the pillar of strength for the whole family during this challenging time. His love and devotion to his wife touched the hearts of the people through his regular updates on social media. It is their love story during the most difficult season of their life. Through his heart-warming account, you will see a glimpse of miracles, answered prayers, and the sustaining love of God. The excerpts about Wilma's condition were written by Perry and were used in the following devotions. In the end, it is still God's will that prevailed. It was not the answer that we wanted. We may not understand the reasons for the many whys, but their life story reminded us that His ways are higher than ours, and His thoughts are not ours. Ultimately, everything happens for His glory and for the greater good. We just have to trust the unconditional love of the Sovereign God. We must keep our hope burning, keep our faith enlightened by God's Word, and let God's love rule our hearts and minds in Christ Jesus our Lord.)*

# DAY 20: OUR FRIEND THE MESSIAH

***"there is a friend who sticks closer than a brother."***
***Proverbs 18:24***

Wilma - She is an example of Proverbs 31 Woman. She is worth more than rubies or any precious stones, silver or gold. She has infectious smiles and laughter. She is beautiful inside and out. It's because she has a grateful heart. Praying is like breathing air to her, and praising God is her way of life. She is one of a kind - my BFF -best friend forever.

On October 8, 2014, Wilma wrote:

Thank You Lord JESUS...

Thank You for Your grace for each day
Your love that endures forever
Your lovingkindness that never ceases
Your amazing grace
Your faithful provision
Your hand of protection
Your wisdom when we need to know what we are doing
Your peace that surpasses all understanding
Your warm embrace when we feel so all alone and lonely
Your faithfulness for each passing day
Your healing for our sickness
Your forgiveness for our sins
Your restoration for our brokenness
Your wholeness for our brokenness

Your provision of family and faithful friends
Your guidance when we need help
Your strength for each day
Your healing on my life (ovarian tumor….)

Thank You, Jesus, for You made it possible for us to be reconciled to our Heavenly Father. Only You can complete us and fill the emptiness that we experience in our lives. Only You can give meaning and purpose to our existence. Only You can bring restoration and wholeness to our brokenness and loss. Only You can love us deeply and unconditionally.

Only You are the Author of Life…Only You…
Only You can bring the blind man's sight.
Only You are called the Prince of Peace.
Only You are God!

Wilma is my best friend. But Wilma and I have our very best friend who loved us first. Another version of Proverbs 18:24 says:

*"Some friendships don't last for long, but there is one loving friend who is joined to your heart closer than any other!" (TPT).* He sacrificed Himself for you and me to give us eternal life. He died on the cross, rose from the dead, went to heaven, and is now seated at the Father's right hand. And He is coming again! Our BBFF – Beloved Best Friend Forever - His name is Yeshua Messiah – JESUS CHRIST, our Lord and Savior!

**Prayer:**

Lord, You are our Best Friend who understands our fears, loves our passions, and keeps our deepest secrets. Your steadfast love helps us to endure our dark and difficult situations in life. Your Holy Word that gives hope and encouragement is like holy kisses in our hearts and whispers of love to our ears. Truly, You are our BBFF!

**Lord, You are our Beloved Best Friend Forever!**

____________________________________________

____________________________________________

____________________________________________

____________________________________________

____________________________________________

____________________________________________

____________________________________________

In Jesus Name, Amen!

***"Greater love has no one than this, than to lay down one's life for his friends. You are My friends if you do whatever I command you… I have called you friends, for all things that I heard from My Father I have made known to you."***
***John 15:13-15***

# DAY 21: THE LORD MY REDEEMER

***"Why are you cast down, O my soul? And why are you disquieted within me? Hope in God, for I shall yet praise Him for the help of His countenance."***
***Psalm 42:5***

*This is a short version of what Wilma wrote for her talk in one of the church group gatherings about few years ago. These still captured the heart and the essence of her message and hopefully will encourage the reader in some ways. – Perry*

## When You Feel Stuck

### Wilma Requina Testimony

Thus far, my life this year has not been how I had hoped and planned. And I am not happy about it.

It's not that I wanted "more;" I just wanted "different."

We can feel stuck when a difficult situation rages into our lives, and we don't like it one bit yet can't escape it. We can feel stuck when it seems we've done everything possible to bring about change of some sort — yet nothing seems to ever change. Or when we're constantly trying to manipulate things to go our way, control things beyond our control or change people, we have no power to change.

I've finally realized that even if it seems justified, I don't have to let discontentment or bitterness poison my heart and mind. I don't have to let the things that are not perfect cause me to take life for granted. I don't have to let unhappiness close my eyes to all the wonderful things God has given me - things that bring me true joy.

All of these challenges brought me to a place where I desire nothing but to hear and listen to God's WORD. I would savor HIS WORD, embrace it, chew it, ruminate it until it becomes so real in my heart and mind. It meant surrendering my "whys" and choosing instead to ask, "Will You help me see You, Lord? Even in this?"

I've come to understand that the Lord longs for me to experience His presence and power at each waking moment, every minute of the day, even in disappointments. He has never left me. He is always with me.

This is exactly what Paul taught in Philippians 4:12; Paul told the church at Philippi, "I know what it is to be in need, and I know what it is to have plenty. I have learned the secret of being content in any and every situation, whether well fed or hungry, whether living in plenty or in want."

He wrote these specific words while sitting in a prison cell. He'd been arrested on false charges by corrupt officials and faced the possibility of execution, yet he wrote that he'd learned to be content with whatever he had. At that moment, he literally had nothing, not even his freedom. How could he feel that way after all he'd been through, more so while in prison? In Philippians 4:13, we find the answer. Paul said, "I can do all this through him who gives me strength." Regardless of his circumstances and despite enduring much persecution and loss, Paul could live with peace and contentment because his heart was right with God.

Life is not always exciting. It's not always easy. It's not always fair. We're all going to feel a sense of unhappiness or discontentment occasionally. But we don't have to stay stuck there. The life we live today is the life God has given us. We can choose to be content and joyful despite our challenges or be the opposite. His Spirit causes me to remain grateful and thankful — STILL!

Let's be careful not to get stuck in our whys. Let's not allow them to leave us blind to His presence, blind to His goodness, blind to His power, blind to the hope we have in Him. Let's not be like the Pharisees — people who could physically see but were blind to the Savior standing before them.

I know this isn't easy. Trust me. I've had situations where I begged God to give me answers. But I realized that instead of Him giving me answers, He's given me Himself.

**Prayer:**

Father God, we might not have all the answers, but we see more hope than ever. Thank You for reminding us that this day holds Your presence, blessings, and comfort. Give us eyes to see You. Help us to be content and learn to live with a heart full of gratitude and love for the life You have given us, no matter what it may look like. You are our YHWH Gaal!

***YHWH Gaal – The Lord Redeemer***
***Read: Isaiah 54:8***

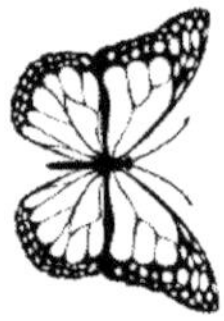

**Lord, You are our Redeemer!**

In Jesus Name, Amen

***"For I know that my Redeemer lives,
And He shall stand at last on the earth;
And after my skin is destroyed, this I know,
That in my flesh I shall see God…"
Job 19:25-27***

***"Christ has redeemed us from the curse of the law…
That the blessing of Abraham might come upon the
Gentiles in Christ Jesus, that we might receive the
promise of the Spirit through faith."
Galatians 3:13-14***

# Day 22: Lord, The Refiner

***"Yea, though I walk through the valley of the shadow of death, I will fear no evil, for You are with me; Your rod and Your staff, they comfort me."***
***Psalm 23:4***

The Lord allows trials and difficulties in life to build our character pleasing to Him. He refines us to be useful in God's Kingdom.

Although we go through fire and water (Psalm 66:10-12):

***"For You, O God, have tested us;***
***You have refined us as silver is refined…***
***You laid affliction on our backs…***
***We went through fire and through water;***
***But You brought us out to rich fulfillment."***

Although the Lord gives us the bread of adversity and the water of affliction (Isaiah 30:20-21):

***"And though the Lord gives you***
***The bread of adversity and the water of affliction…***
***Your ears shall hear a word behind you, saying,***
***"This is the way, walk in it,"***

Although we are being tested in the furnace of affliction (Isaiah 48:10-12):

***"Behold, I have refined you, but not as silver;***
***I have tested you in the furnace of affliction.***
***For My own sake, for My own sake, I will do it…***
***I am He, I am the First, I am also the Last."***

We shall come forth as gold (Job 23:10):

***"But He knows the way that I take;***
***When He has tested me, I shall come forth as gold."***

**March 30, 2020**: Wilma was taken to the hospital when she tested positive for covid-19. She needed to be on oxygen support. She also had pneumonia.

**April 2020:** Wilma was intubated, which has kept her oxygen saturation level at 98%. Doctors sedated and paralyzed her to allow the ventilator to do the breathing for her. Wilma's lungs have been badly hit by the virus. The scan images showed that she had a severe stroke that may have been caused by blood clotting, and she might not wake up. The family was told that if things got worse at that point, she would pass away. Her trajectory was downward, and she was at the end of the line. Perry was asked if he needed Wilma to have the last rites done.

**May 2020:** Wilma's tracheostomy was successful. Her condition remained stable, but she was on and off the ventilator. Sadly, the prognosis based on the CT scan was that she might not wake up at all. As Perry wrote, "This news is heartbreaking. The only thing holding me up right now is the belief that with God, nothing is impossible. I believe in a miracle.

I'm looking forward to seeing Wilma wake up…"

After less than a week, during the Family's Facetime, her eyes opened wide for the entire video call. She was asked to look up to say, "Yes, she recognizes them," and she quickly did! The family encouraged her to continue her trust in God, to not be anxious or afraid, and to never lose hope that God will restore whatever they have lost through covid-19 (time with family and friends, her mobility and functioning, etc.). Worship songs were played, and prayers were uttered to lift her spirits up. Before the end of the month, she was off the ventilator, breathing on her own.

**June 2020**: Wilma suffered from what is called a locked-in syndrome. She was conscious and cognitively intact but was unable to communicate because of her paralysis. Video calls from her family have been limited to only once per week. Sometimes, the family would simply talk to her over the phone. They hoped and prayed that they would visit her in person regularly because touching her would be therapeutic since touch is her love language.

Wilma celebrated her birthday in the hospital, and her family was able to visit her in person. This was her first time seeing any of her family in person since being taken to the hospital about two and a half months ago. "I could say that the entire visit was not found wanting with emotional moments. For us to touch and hold her was very special indeed." Perry said. They set up an iPhone in her room to do Facetime daily. They also planned with the hospital's interfaith chaplain to regularly visit Wilma for prayer, Bible reading, and the playing of worship songs. The family was approved to see her in person once a week, though it was tough to see her writhe in pain. From time to time, her leg and arm muscles would contract, which caused her excruciating pain. Only with a copious amount of grace and inner strength from God would she endure the untold physical pain and emotional anguish that she went through.

**Prayer:**

Lord, You are the Good Shepherd who will lead us through the valleys of life – disappointments, discouragements, dilemmas, and dark and difficult days. We do not have to fear because this is the road to higher ground in our walk with God. You refine us and mold us into the kind of person that You want us to be. You are our Tsaraph!

***Tsaraph – Hebrew word meaning to smelt, refine; to test (and prove true) smelter, refiner, goldsmith***

**Lord, may You find me true to my faith and help me pass the test:**

____________________________________________________________

____________________________________________________________

____________________________________________________________

____________________________________________________________

____________________________________________________________

____________________________________________________________

____________________________________________________________

In Jesus Name, Amen!

***"He will sit as a refiner and a purifier of silver;***
***He will purify the sons of Levi,***
***And purge them as gold and silver,***
***That they may offer to the Lord***
***An offering in righteousness."***
***Malachi 3:3***

***"The Lord gave, and the Lord has taken away; Blessed be the name of the Lord."***
***Job 1:21***

# Day 23: The Most High God

***"Blessed be Abram of God Most High,***
***Possessor of heaven and earth…"***
***Genesis 14:19***

**Perry Requina Testimony**

Just scribbling and babbling…

Being told Wilma wouldn't wake up at all was too overwhelming and shocking to ingest. Strangely, though, I feel like it's only now that I'm slowly recovering from the shock and re-establishing my bearing. In the last few days, I was feeling uncharacteristically off. I have been shedding quite a significant number of tears, fighting through some persistent negative thoughts, and struggling to sleep through some restless nights.

I miss my wife. Wilma and I have never been separated this long since we got married. Feelings of regrets hounded me: they should have been and could have been what ifs and if I only could. I was worried about how difficult it would be for Wilma, me, and the rest of my family if she lay asleep on a hospital bed for the rest of her life.

I felt disappointed. It seemed as if my prayer for Wilma's healing had fallen on deaf ears. I felt confused, not knowing whether I should pray, "Lord, not my will, but yours be done," as Jesus did at Gethsemane, or pray, "Lord, I won't let go unless you bless me," as Jacob did at Bethel.

I chose to stay busy and not allow myself to be ruled by the dictates of my emotions – especially negative ones. I tried to make my day as productive and fulfilling as possible. But when the night falls, I lay in bed without Wilma by my side. The room felt cold, in need of the warmth of her presence. The house seemed dull. It felt like a void could only be filled by her effervescent personality and the sweet aroma of her cooking and baking. Lord, when will this parting end? When will my wife be finally home? Or will she?

I've often wondered how I'd be able to walk through this valley of grief with my head remaining straight and my feet continually grounded had God not reached down to comfort and encourage me. I have never gotten so easily emotional just as I had been in the past few days. I shed a lot of tears, indeed. Yet, ironically, they were mostly tears of comfort rather than tears of sorrow, tears of faith and confidence rather than despair, a kind of trust that is based on knowing God and His character. He is good, and He is in control.

I was sad but not depressed, worried but not anxious, disappointed but not discouraged, and confused but not disillusioned. Incredible as it may sound, I had peace in the middle of a tumultuous storm.

I will meet with the doctors this afternoon, but I have no idea if I will be hearing good news. I have confidence in the doctors' knowledge and competencies and their desire to serve Wilma. But my full confidence is in my God, who is All-powerful and All-knowing. He loves Wilma much more than I love her. He is good, righteous, and true. Nothing evil nor malice proceed from Him. He is sovereign. He acts according to His divine will and pleasure.

Frankly, my dilemma is this: I am totally clueless about God's will for Wilma. I don't know if God's will be to send her home to us, or to make the hospital or any form of hospice her home, or to take her with Him to His celestial home. I know that in all three scenarios, He will make all things work for good (See Romans 8:28).

Greater still, I know that He has invited me to come boldly into His throne of grace that I may find help in time of need (Hebrews 4:16). He also dares me to ask Him that my joy may be full (John 16:24). This is what I ask of God that my joy may be full: that Wilma will come home, alive and well, as if covid had never happened.

Needless to say, I'm careful not to presume that this is God's specific will for Wilma at this point. I'm careful not to put God in a box, especially in a box I had created. But unless God reveals otherwise, I will hold on to this box and keep believing for a miracle. I'm not being naïve nor fatalistic. But unless God reveals unequivocally that the box He had prepared for Wilma is different from what I have in mind, I will keep expecting her to come home to us alive and well.

I believe that God, being the good Father that He is, will not give me a stone if I ask for bread, a snake if I ask for fish (Matthew 7:9). I come before God like a child asking his loving father to give him the desire of his heart. I come before my Father in heaven, asking and believing for a miracle for Wilma. Thank You for encouraging me to keep on believing in a miracle. Even more so, thank You for believing in me.

**Prayer:**

Lord, You are the Most High, All-powerful, All-knowing, and All-present God. You are righteous in all Your ways, and You never make mistakes. You deserve our adoration, worship, and praise. We exalt You and bless Your name as the One with the final say in our lives. Help us to completely trust Your sovereign will. You are our El Elyon.

***El Elyon – The Most High God***
***Read: Genesis 14:18-24: Psalm 97***

**Lord, there is no one like You!**

In Jesus Name, Amen!

***"I will cry out to God Most High,***
***To God who performs all things for me."***
***Psalm 57:2***

***"… I blessed the Most High and praised and honored***
***Him who lives forever…"***
***Daniel 4:34***

***"For You, Lord,*** are ***most high above all the earth;***
***You are exalted far above all gods."***
***Psalm 97:9***

# DAY 24: THE SOVEREIGN LORD

***"The pains of death surrounded me, and the pangs of Sheoul laid hold of me; I found trouble and sorrow. Then I called upon the name of the Lord: "O Lord, I implore You, deliver my soul!"***
***Psalm 116: 3-4***

**August 2020:** "Wilma's fever could be because of her bed sore; though it has not gone worse, it has not gone better. Wilma had periods of posturing (decerebrating), which caused her excruciating pain. They would give her stronger pain medications to help her cope. Neuro-wise, Wilma would respond appropriately to yes or no questions. When asked to blink 4 times, she complied; blink 3 times, she complied, and then, finally, twice, and she blinked twice. Amazing indeed! When she saw the video of her son's hamster, hoping to evoke laughter from her, she started crying instead. She had shed tears and got emotional at times, but that was the first time the family saw her cry for a significantly longer period. She was groaning and had a facial expression that was characterized as that of someone crying. She cried for about 20 minutes or so. You just cannot imagine the loneliness, longing, sadness, helplessness, fear, anxiety, discouragement, exasperation, and other negative emotions that have beset her. Maybe crying is good for her, as it allows her to release whatever emotional distress and tension she's feeling and also helps her flush out some neurotoxins in her brain. Regardless of how trivial and insignificant they may seem, her progress was still progress," Perry said.

"We had a chat with the infectious diseases doctor that's looking after Wilma. She gave us a general picture of how Wilma is and could be as plainly and directly as she could. Even though I found her quite tactful, she did pose some very tough questions for us to seriously consider. To say it was a difficult conversation to be heard is an understatement."

"To cut our long conversation short, it centered largely on Wilma's pressure ulcer. She said she was worried for Wilma because she doesn't think her bed sore will heal. Thus, her wound would continue to remain open, and her bone would be exposed. Infection will be a continued cause for major concern. This can prove to be fatal, given the resilient nature of bacteria. She thinks that Wilma is at the halfway mark in her fight against infections. Given Wilma's condition, the doctor thinks that we're not on the winning side."

"The doctor's prognosis is based on facts and medical science. I don't find her at fault for doing so. But I choose to see Wilma's condition through the eyes of faith."

"Four months ago, we were told by the doctors that Wilma was losing her fight against covid and that her passing away was very much imminent. She beat that prognosis. About three months ago, her doctor told us that she wasn't going to regain consciousness. Again, she beat that prognosis," narrated Perry.

**Prayer:**

Lord, You are in control, and all things work together for good and for Your glory. We surrender to Your perfect will and eternal purposes with confidence and joy in our hearts. You act with supreme authority and absolute power to do what pleases You. Give us a heart that is united to Your heart, knowing that You are Sovereign in all things – over our abundance and famine, our health and sickness, and life and death. You are our YHWH Adonai!

*Adonai- Hebrew word that translates as "Lord"*
*of "Lord Master" from its derivation "sovereignty"*
*Read: Psalm 103*

**Lord, we rest on Your Sovereignty:**

_______________________________________________

_______________________________________________

_______________________________________________

_______________________________________________

_______________________________________________

_______________________________________________

_______________________________________________

In Jesus Name, Amen!

*"Ah, Lord God! Behold, You have made the heavens and the earth by Your great power and outstretched arm. There is nothing too hard for you... You are great in counsel and mighty in work..."*
*Jeremiah 32:17-19*

# DAY 25: THE LORD, MY LIGHT

*"The Lord* is *my light and my salvation;*
*Whom shall I fear?*
*The Lord* is *the strength of my life;*
*Of whom shall I be afraid?"*
*Psalm 27:1*

**September 2020**: Wilma's vitals are generally good. Her bed sore is still on stage 3 but was improving. Praise God! Although Wilma still has no control over her body, she can still respond to "Yes or No" questions by blinking. A piece of welcoming news – Wilma will be transferred to a complex care facility. "WOW! Three months ago, we were told that Wilma did not qualify as a candidate for rehab. A month and a half ago, we were told that she wasn't going to survive. But now, they're talking about moving her to complex care. We told her medical team that we trust their expertise and competence during our meetings. All we ask of them is for them to attend to her the best they know how, and we'll pray the best we know how." Perry wrote on his Facebook update.

**October 2020:** Wilma was moved to Parkwood Rehab Center. Her transfer to Parkwood is a miracle in itself, as she was considered not a candidate for rehab after undergoing a series of tests. Then, a month later, doctors feared that she was losing her fight against infection, so much so that the medical team met with the family not only to discuss her condition but also to determine the DNR decision (do not resuscitate). Wilma, in the rehab phase of her journey toward recovery, had defied grim prognoses. However, she still needs to battle her way toward full recovery daily.

**December 2020**: Wilma did speech therapy five to six times a week to establish communication through a computer tablet by using her eyes or pressing a button. She was regularly wheeled out of her room to join a group session with other patients.

"Last Sunday, we got to have some perfect laughing moments during my visit. Wilma and I had not really laughed together since her hospitalization. She still has to make sounds, though. But it was wonderful nevertheless. I told her I was not going to give up on her. Then I asked her to promise me not to give up on herself. I asked her to move her right thumb to say "yes." She did!" Perry said, keeping the hope alive.

**Prayer:**

Lord, You are the world's Light, and You have no darkness. May Your light of hope shine and illuminate our dark and dreary path. May the light of Your Word encourage our lonely and weary hearts. May the light of Your countenance be seen in us when we face difficult and painful trials of life. Help us to walk as children of light so those who are dying and needing the Savior will seek and find the Light of the world- Yeshua Messiah!

***Ani Hu HaOhr HaOlam Hazeh-***
***From Orthodox Jewish Bible meaning***
***"I Am the Light of the world" John 8:12***
***Read: Matthew 5; 1 John 1; Isaiah 49***

**Lord, You are the Light of the World; illuminate our path:**

_______________________________________________

_______________________________________________

_______________________________________________

_______________________________________________

_______________________________________________

_______________________________________________

_______________________________________________

In Jesus Name, Amen!

***"… When I sit in darkness, the Lord will be a light to me." Micah 7:8***

***"That was the true Light which gives light to every man coming into the world." John 1:9***

***"Then Jesus spoke to them again, saying, "I am the light of the world. He who follows Me shall not walk in darkness, but have the light of life." John 8:12***

# DAY 26: THE LORD, OUR MAKER

***"Oh come, let us worship and bow down; let us kneel before the Lord our Maker."***
***Psalm 95:6***

**March 2021**: Exactly a year ago, 911 was called, and Wilma was taken by an ambulance and brought straight to the hospital. She has not been home since then. She fought one medical condition (and crisis!) after another. She suffered from locked-in syndrome, and her communication was mostly limited to answering yes or no questions. Wilma cried, laughed, and reacted during interactions. She responded to commands and instructions the best she could. Her progress had been generally slow. But she had come a long way compared to where she was from a year ago. Her indomitable spirit and resolute faith in God refuse to be held hostage by her physical condition and limitations.

"We try to keep her going, but I do admit that there have been many times that it's her who keeps me going. I want to express my deepest and sincerest gratitude to everyone of you who has diligently and tirelessly prayed for Wilma and us, her family. Thanks for your generous expressions of love and concern for her welfare and ours. You have made our journey a lot easier and the burden more bearable. May God bless you all richly," states Perry.

**June 2021**: Ontario province was placed on strict lockdown two months ago due to covid. Hospital visits and window visits have also been shut down. Six weeks later, the family was given the chance to visit her. "We have been praying for this for weeks!" Perry said.

"Today is Wilma's birthday, and Parkwood is gracious enough to bless me with an extra visit. I tried to encourage her to keep fighting, hoping and praying. I asked her to look up to affirm that she was indeed not giving up. She did. I visited Wilma for her birthday with my older son a year ago. On my 2nd visit, it was the first time I saw her awake and conscious since leaving home. My 1st visit was with my two younger children about a month prior, but she was still in a coma at that time. A lot has happened in a span of 15 months. Needless to say, Wilma's progress is not only a testament to God's faithfulness but also to her indomitable fighting spirit.

We're looking forward to the time when she's finally home. In the meantime, we'll keep fighting, hoping, and praying." Perry added.

**July 2021:** About 3 months ago, Wilma's speech pathologist, thinking outside the box, decided to present Wilma's case to the people at the Assistive Device Program of Ontario in the hope that she will be accepted into the program. The ADP is mostly for people with ALS and cerebral palsy. Thankfully, they were gracious enough to consider Wilma, assess her, and finally accept her into the program. The communication device is called Tobii Dynavox 1-13. Wilma did a great job when she was asked to focus on different letters that the device would then pronounce once gazed long enough. In the days ahead, they will have her spell words or focus on preprogrammed phases or sentences, making communication with her healthcare providers and her family much easier. A program called Communicator 5 can be installed on the device, allowing Wilma access to Facebook, Skype texting, Netflix, YouTube, etc. A switching device, which will be attached to the Tobii 1-13, was also sent by ADP. It is called a neuronode switch. This is so highly sensitive that it can be triggered simply by using eyebrows or by blinking. This switch will provide her with another option for controlling the Tobii in addition to eye gaze. The session took more than an hour, and Wilma was visibly exhausted. But she showed a lot of grit and determination. She really wanted this device to work.

"I couldn't be prouder of her. We're still praying for Wilma's full healing, that she would be able to talk and walk. But for now, we're grateful for whatever blessings God has afforded us. Thank You, Lord, for the Tobii I-13. Don't be surprised, though, if a few months from now, Wilma is back on Facebook! This is really awesome!" mused Perry.

**Prayer:**

Father, You are the Maker of heaven and earth. You created this world out of nothing. You formed us in our mother's womb through Your divine action for a purpose. So, while we wait for Your plan to unfold, strengthen us and give us hope. While we anticipate our prayers to be answered, give us peace that passes all understanding. While we eagerly await Your miraculous healing power, prepare our hearts for Your holy will and desire. We trust You, our YHWH Osenu.

***YHWH Osenu – The Lord our Maker;***
***He transforms His creation to His desire***
***Read: Psalm 95***

**Lord, our Maker, reveal to us Your plan and purpose:**

In Jesus Name, Amen!

***"Out of the depths I have cried to You, O Lord;***
***Lord, hear my voice! Let Your ears be attentive***
***To the voice of my supplications…***
***I wait for the Lord, my soul waits,***
***And in His word I do hope."***
***Psalm 130:1-5***

***"But those who wait on the Lord***
***shall renew their strength; They shall mount up***
***with wings like eagles, they shall run and not be weary,***
***they shall walk and not faint."***
***Isaiah 40:31***

# Day 27: God with us

***"For unto us a Child is born, unto us a Son is given; and the government will be upon His shoulder. And His name will be called Wonderful, Counselor, Mighty God, Everlasting Father, Prince of Peace."***
***Isaiah 9:6***

**November 2021**: Wilma has been using the assistive communication device, TOBII S13, with programmed personalized vocabularies. Her speech therapists noted that Wilma generally did well during her sessions.

Sometimes, she seemed unresponsive and not as interactive during the visits. There would be times when she seemed rather sad, and there were times when she would laugh, even laugh really hard. She would laugh at jokes or funny videos and pictures, and sometimes even with random comments. She would oblige when asked to close her eyes. Her response/reaction time would be rapid, just like in any normal interaction. By large, her disposition remained positive.

**December 2021**: Wilma was transferred to the respirology unit at Victoria Hospital for respiratory issues. Before the transfer, she was being treated at Parkwood for suspected pneumonia, her third incidence in the last two months. But unlike the previous incidents, her temperature won't go down even after being administered a stronger antibiotic. Hence, I decided to have her transferred.

"Ironic as it may sound. I wish you all a very Merry Christmas. Our Christmas may not be what we wish for, but God has come to be with us. This is worth celebrating. I know that the God who is with me and my family through this difficult chapter of our lives is also with Wilma in her hospital room," Perry said.

**Prayer:**

Lord, may we reflect on the true reason for the season – the promised Messiah was born in Bethlehem to give us hope and peace. As we remember the birth of Christ, fill us with joy and love that will sustain us. As we reflect on the meaning and importance of Christmas, may we not give up but continue to trust in the exceeding power and the atoning sacrifices of Jesus, our Savior - Immanu-El!

***Immanu-El – God with us***
***Read: Matthew 1-2; Luke 1-2: Micah 5:2; Isaiah 7:14***

**Lord Jesus, You are God our Savior!**

In Jesus Name, Amen!

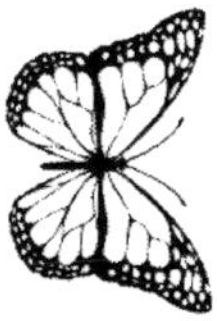

*"And she will bring forth a Son, and you shall call His name JESUS, for He will save His people from their sins."*
*So, all this was done that it might be fulfilled which was spoken by the Lord through the prophet, saying: "Behold, the virgin shall be with child, and bear a Son, and they shall call His name Immanuel," which is translated, "God with us."*
*Matthew 1:21-23*

*"Therefore, the Lord Himself will give you a sign: Behold, the virgin shall conceive and bear a Son, and shall call His name Immanuel"*
*Isaiah 7:14*

# Day 28: The Everlasting God

***"Have you not known? Have you not heard?***
***The everlasting God, the Lord,***
***The Creator of the ends of the earth,***
***Neither faints nor is weary.***
***His understanding is unsearchable."***
***Isaiah 40:28***

**January 2022**: Sadly, there had been an outbreak in Wilma's unit, and when they tested the patients, Wilma tested positive. Wilma had been double vaccinated and had a booster shot, too. But given her condition, she was highly vulnerable.

**March 2022:** After two years in the hospital, Wilma remained to be generally stable. I have seen her laugh a couple of times lately, but I still have to see her have a hearty laugh and make that laughing sound like she used to while at Parkwood. Hopefully, as she regains her strength and her disposition improves, we'll see her smile and laugh more often."

**May 2022**: Wilma is back at Parkwood, a complex-care facility. Neurologically, she was still able to move her eyes and eyebrows. She could still press hard with her right thumb but not much with her left. She can smile as requested from time to time.

"This weekend, she had a very hearty laugh. I haven't seen or heard her laugh that hard in the past 5-6 months. Last week, my daughter noticed Wilma twitching her left leg. She asked her to do it again, and she complied. I also asked her to move her leg during one of my visits. After many failed attempts, she finally moved her right foot, not her left leg. Thanks for your continued prayers and support. Happy Mother's Day to all mothers!" revealed Perry.

**June 2022**: Wilma's vitals have been stable for the last two months. But then, on her third birthday in the hospital, she had a temperature that was in the high 38s. They immediately tested her for covid. The results were negative.

**July 2022**: "Just spent my birthday with my very strong and beautiful wife, Wilma. Birthdays, holidays, and other special occasions evoke mixed emotions in me. On the one hand, I'm happy and blessed to celebrate them with my loved ones, but on the other hand, I wish Wilma was around to celebrate it with me just as we did in the past two decades. Her being in the hospital leaves a gaping hole that only she can fill. Aside from simply celebrating them, what helps keep me emotionally and mentally grounded is that I commemorate these occasions. I mark it with a stubborn resolve to continue to trust God no matter what. I mark it with renewed faith and hope that Wilma will one day celebrate these occasions with me just as she used to, complete with her beaming smile and unabashed laughter. Yesterday's Our Daily Bread devotion was entitled "Live Like Your Healed." After expounding on it a bit, I asked her to blink twice if she still believed for her miracle to happen. She blinked twice. I couldn't be more blessed to commemorate my birthday with my strong, beautiful wife, Wilma," narrated Perry.

**August 2022**: Wilma's vitals were good. She just returned from Victoria Hospital, where she was treated for infection. She was at the hospital for 10 days, then back at Parkwood. She had visits from friends and family in the past two months. The visits did make her very emotional. She was both sad and happy. She clearly felt very much loved.

**Prayer:**

Almighty and everlasting Father, we worship and glorify Your name. Your great love towards us is as high as the highest heavens and as deep as the deepest sea. Because of Your mercy and grace, our sins are forgiven and removed from us as far as the East is from the West. You are compassionate and gracious; slow to anger and abounding in love. You are truly our El Olam!

***El Olam- Everlasting God or Eternal God The Hebrew word olam means "for a long time, always, forever. "El Olam" reveals God as "the Everlasting God", without beginning or end.***
***Read: Psalm 103***

**Lord, thank You for Your everlasting love:**

In Jesus Name, Amen!

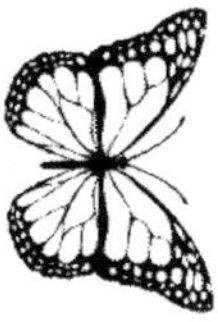

*"Then Abraham... called on the name of the Lord,*
*the Everlasting God."*
*Genesis 21:33*

*"For as the heavens are high above the earth,*
So *great is His mercy toward those who fear Him;*
*As far as the east is from the west,*
So *far has He removed our transgressions from us.*
*As a father pities* his *children,*
So *the Lord pities those who fear Him.*
*For He knows our frame;*
*He remembers that we* are *dust."*
*Psalm 103:11-14*

# Day 29: The Victorious God

***"Remember how short my time is; …***
***What man can live and not see death?***
***Can he deliver his life from the power of grave?"***
***Psalm 89:47-48***

**September 2022:** I got a call from Victoria Hospital. I was informed that Wilma's blood work result looked terrible and that sending her to the ICU was pointless. Wilma was dying. It was the third time that the doctors told the family she was dying. The first was in April 2020 and then again in July 2020. But this time, it was different. She has been suffering for two and a half years. It was suggested that they would switch her to comfort care as opposed to sending her to ICU. I argued and told them that 25 years ago, Wilma prayed to a neighbor who was in the same exact condition as hers - dying. She miraculously survived and eventually got healed, and she is still alive today. The doctors sent her to the ICU.

"But deep inside, I am confused. Will sending her to the ICU prolong her suffering? Or will it give her a fighting chance to live? I did not know what to do. I did not know what to pray. I asked God to guide me and give me clarity. And He did; no more Parkwood. That became very clear. That became my prayer. Either she is going home to be with us in London or with the Father in heaven. I shared this with Wilma and asked her to squeeze with her right thumb if she agreed, and she squeezed. She mustered all her declining strength to give faint squeezes just to tell me she concurred. She agreed. She is going home. All my burdens and heaviness were lifted. I was comforted by the fact that Wilma was at peace. My wife was ready to go home."

"Wilma breathed her last breath. But then, an amazing thing happened. She smiled for two, probably three seconds. That was beautiful! In her dying seconds, she managed to smile. We were crying but ecstatic and dumbfounded. How amazing it was to see her smiling. She was not only at peace, but she was happy! She saw something wonderful, so beautiful that she could not keep smiling! I could imagine her right now, smiling in the presence of the Father in heaven. Yes, laughing, giggling, and more laughter, bigger smiles," as narrated by Perry during Wilma's viewing service.

**Prayer:**

Father, our glorious King, and Master, Your Word said the perishable had been clothed with the imperishable and the mortal with immortality, as it is written, "Death has been swallowed up in victory." Thank You that our departed loved ones who professed You as their Lord and Savior are now rejoicing in Your presence. We pray that just as our Lord Jesus Christ overcame death when He rose from the dead on the third day, completing His Atoning sacrifice on the cross, our hope is alive because of His resurrection. Precious are those who died in the Lord because Your Son redeemed them. You will usher them in Your presence and live with You in eternity. Lord, for those of us who are still in pain, sorrow, and difficulty, may we always be reminded of this truth. You are victorious by conquering death. We can also say we are victorious and more than conquerors because You are our YHWH Nissi!

***YHWH Nissi - meaning 'The Lord Our Banner'or 'God my Victory.' The Hebrew word 'Nissi' means banner, as in battle flag, protective covering, and victory.***
***Read: Exodus 17:15***

**Lord, thank You that there is victory in You:**

_______________________________________________
_______________________________________________
_______________________________________________
_______________________________________________
_______________________________________________
_______________________________________________
_______________________________________________

In Jesus Name, Amen!

***"So when this corruptible has put on incorruption, and this mortal has put on immortality, then shall be brought to pass the saying that is written:***
***"Death is swallowed up in victory."***
***"O Death, where* is *your sting? O Hades, where* is *your victory?"...But thanks* be *to God, who gives us the victory through our Lord Jesus Christ."***
***1 Corinthians 15:54-57***
***Read: I Corinthians 15; Isaiah 25:8-9; Hosea 13:14***

# DAY 30: THE RESURRECTION AND THE LIFE

***"For to me, to live is Christ, and to die is gain."***
***Philippians 1:21***

**September 20, 2022**: Wilma was promoted in heaven.

She fought the good fight of faith for two and a half years. She finished her race with flying colors. Wilma's struggles paraded the power of God in social media, as Perry gave a regular update on how Wilma and her family trusted and believed in God's sovereign plan. They were selected to struggle for God's glory. They suffered for His sake so the world would see how God loves us. The Lord will always be there for us in whatever struggles, difficulties, and challenges we face. Perry fulfilled his promise to Wilma that "for better, for worse, for richer, for poorer, in sickness and in health, until death do us part." Similarly, the Father showed His unconditional love to us that He gave His only begotten Son to die on the cross for our sins so we can have eternal life.

Wilma smiled! The Bible says, ***"In Your presence is fullness of joy." (Psalm 16:11).***

Wilma smiled when the gates of heaven opened for her and met the lover of her soul face to face. I could imagine her very ecstatic, hugging the Lord while hearing Him say to her, "Well done, my good and faithful friend. Welcome, my child!" And the new journey with The Father in eternity begins!

**Prayer:**

Lord, thank You for Your comfort and peace when our loved one left the earthly body to be with the Savior in eternity. Lord, no matter how hard and difficult it is to lose Wilma - the best friend of all, the best mother for her children, and the best wife to Bro. Perry, we know we can be glad, thankful, and hopeful. We can be glad because God promised to give eternal life to those who believe in the Lord Jesus. Wilma believed and accepted You as her personal Lord & Savior. She is now in Your presence… met Jesus face to face, the Author and Finisher of our faith, the Lover of our soul. We can be glad because Your Word says that in Your presence, "there shall be no more death, mourning crying, or pain. We can be hopeful because He who promised is faithful, and all Your promises are Yes and Amen. That one day, there will be a grand reunion in heaven for those who believed in the saving power of the cross. That is our appointed time; we will meet our loved ones who accepted You as their Lord and Savior. We can be thankful because no matter how lonely it is not to hear Wilma's laugh and giggles, no matter how we miss her cakes, her dancing and jumping, how incomplete it is without her presence on special occasions like Thanksgiving, Birthdays and Christmas, we know that You will be with us, You will comfort us and give us peace that passes all understanding… that You are in the midst of our pain and grief as You promised, You will "never leave us nor forsake us." Thank You for what Wilma taught us – she taught us to pray without ceasing… Lord, thank You for her family, her church family, and all her friends worldwide who fought the battle with her on their knees in prayer… Thank You for what Wilma showed us – she showed us perseverance under trial, and having stood the test, she received the crown of life that the Lord has promised to those who love him (James 1:12). She fought the good fight of faith and emerged victorious and more than a conqueror in Christ. Lord, I could imagine when You welcomed her in Your loving arms, hearing You say, “Well done, my good and faithful daughter and friend.” Thank You that Wilma helped us to believe that “the best is yet to come.” We know and believe, beyond any doubt, that Your power and love will never fail us. The best is yet to come. Thank You for Wilma’s life and the legacy she left behind. Her love and memories will be forever imprinted in our hearts. Wilma, you are unique, incomparable, and unparalleled. We love you! Lord, thank You for the strength and tenacity that You have given Perry to hold fast to their marriage vows – the promise to love, honor, and cherish each other as long as they both shall live. Comfort us, cover us with Your grace and mercy, and surround us with Your peace. You alone are our refuge and strength. May our life be like Wilma’s life, filled with thanksgiving and praise for Your countless blessings, full of love in You and hope in Your promises. Truly, this is the celebration of your wondrous working power in the life of Wilma and her family. Lord, we praise and glorify your name in the mighty name of Jesus Christ, Amen.

(Prayer during Wilma’s Celebration of Life in October 2022).

**Lord, thank You that there is life after death:**

_______________________________________________
_______________________________________________
_______________________________________________
_______________________________________________
_______________________________________________
_______________________________________________
_______________________________________________

In Jesus Name, Amen!

***"Jesus said to her, "I am the resurrection and the life. He who believes in Me, though he may die, he shall live. And whoever lives and believes in Me shall never die. Do you believe this?"***
***John 11:25-26***

***"Who shall separate us from the love of Christ? Shall tribulation, or distress, or persecution, or famine, or nakedness, or peril, or sword? …***
***Yet in all these things we are more than conquerors through Him who loved us."***
***Romans 8:35, 37***

***"You number my wanderings; Put my tears into Your bottle; Are they not in Your book?"***
***Psalm 56:8***

## DAY 31: THE GOD ALMIGHTY

***"Weeping may endure for a night, But joy comes in the morning."***
***Psalm 30:5***

**Perry Requina Testimony**

25 years ago, Wilma and I celebrated our marriage with friends and loved ones. Before covid, we looked forward to celebrating our silver wedding anniversary with friends and loved ones, but God has other plans. Our marriage wasn't perfect. It wasn't smooth sailing. But it was both a venue and an avenue for expressing and experiencing God's unconditional and unwavering love. To say "I miss her terribly is an understatement." I wish she were here to celebrate our 25th wedding anniversary. But God has other plans. One day, I'll understand why things happened the way they did. I'll see God's plan and how faithful He has always been. I take solace in the fact that his plans are better than mine. His ways are higher than mine. His will for both Wilma and me is always for our best, nothing less, nothing else.

**A Sentimental Journey**

In March 2023, when I was in the Philippines, I decided to visit the places where our love story started, blossomed, and then finally blessed in a church wedding. I have never shed so many tears since Wilma's funeral. But I felt I needed to do it as part of my grieving and mourning process. A lot of things have changed. The following are insights learned from the visits: 1. The Change: Wilma's office in the admin building was torn down for renovations. The building where her other office used to be was also torn down to make way for a new and bigger structure. The insight: The lady who loved to smile, laugh, sing, dance, pray, praise, worship, cook, bake, etc., and confined to a hospital bed for 2 1/2 years is finally free to enjoy a much better life in eternity unfettered by the limitations of her paralyzed earthly body. Wilma is gone, but her body has been changed from corruptible to incorruptible. 2. The change: The gazebo we used as a backdrop for our wedding photo shoot was old and decrepit, but it was still standing. The insight: The gazebo may be ugly and tattered, but it stood the test of time, inclement weather, and neglect. Wilma suffered from locked-in syndrome for 2 1/2 years. However, despite her seemingly hapless condition, she still managed to laugh, smile, interact, say "I love you" or "Amen" with her eyes, and actively participate in her therapy sessions. Her inner strength and character shone brightly in what should have been the darkest period of her life. 3. The change: The familiar places are still around, but Wilma is not. I was alone when I shopped at the thrift store arcade she used to frequent and ate in the restaurant where we had our first date. She wasn't there at the park where we used to go with our kids. The insight: This is the most difficult part of the trip. Getting used to living in Canada without her is difficult, and being in places filled with her memories was challenging. Needless to say, this is part and parcel of the grieving process - learning to accept the fact that she is gone and learning to create new memories with the family and friends who are still around. Wilma's death left a gaping hole that only she can fill. I know the healing and grieving process will take time. But with God's comforting presence and grace, healing will come.

**Prayer:**

Lord, You are my All-Sufficient One! With You, I am complete. I fully yield my life to You. You are a loving and Sovereign God whose grace and mercy abound. You are faithful to heal the brokenhearted and bind up our wounds. Thank You, El Shaddai!

***El Shaddai – God Almighty***
***All Sufficient God, The God of More Than Enough***
***Read: Job 1, 2 and 42***

**Lord, I surrender all:**

____________________________________________________

____________________________________________________

____________________________________________________

____________________________________________________

____________________________________________________

____________________________________________________

In Jesus Name, Amen!

***"The Lord gave, and the Lord has taken away; Blessed be the name of the Lord." Job 1:21***

***"And we know that all things work together for good to those who love God, to those who are the called according to His purpose."***
***Romans 8:28***

***"And He said to me, "My grace is sufficient for you, For My strength is made perfect in weakness…"***
***2 Corinthians 12:9***

***"… the Lord appeared to Abram and said to him, "I am Almighty God; walk before Me and be blameless."***
***Genesis 17:1***

# ABOUT THE AUTHOR OF SALVATION

***"And having been perfected, He became the author of eternal salvation to all who obey Him."***
***Hebrews 5:9***

**Message by Pastor Ian Opiniano**

God's plan of salvation starts and ends with Him. In theological terms, this *monergistic* work of God means that we contribute nothing to our salvation except the sin that made it necessary. Yet this reality should not be a point of debate as it is often viewed, but rather a monument of hope and freedom to the believer. It describes a salvation planned by the Father from before the foundations of the world, a salvation that the Son willingly paid for at the cross, and a salvation ensured by the sealing of the Holy Spirit. In other words, God alone planned, paid, and protected it.

Knowing that God is the Author and Perfecter of our faith frees us from a life driven by works and reveals the riches of God's grace. For it is by grace–God's unmerited favour alone we inherit this salvation, and not by human works or good intentions. The only requirement for those who desire this salvation is to *believe.* This belief simply trusts that the death of Jesus Christ on the cross was sufficient to appease the wrath of God towards our sins and that only in Him can we find a relationship with the Father.

The most important thing is to have that personal relationship with the Lord – accepting Jesus as our Lord and Savior. He promised eternal life to those who believe.

Receiving this free gift is as easy as "**ABC.**"

**A** – Accept that you are a sinner in need of saving

**B**-- Believe in your heart that Jesus' death and resurrection is sufficient for your salvation

**C** – Call to God in prayer

**Prayer:**

God, have mercy on me, a sinner. I recognize that I do not deserve anything but Your wrath–the punishment for my sin, which is hell. But I believe and trust in Your way for salvation–the way paid for by Jesus' death on the cross and assured by His resurrection. Thank You for loving me and making a way for us to have a relationship. By Your grace, be the Lord of my life, and help me to follow You in Jesus name. Amen.

***"For God so loved the world***
***That He gave His only begotten Son,***
***that whoever believes in Him should not perish but have everlasting life."***
***John 3:16***

***"For all have sinned and fall short of the glory of God"***
***Romans 3:23***

***"For the wages of sin is death, but the gift of God is eternal life in Christ Jesus our Lord."***
***Romans 6:23***

***"that if you confess with your mouth the Lord Jesus and believe in your heart that God has raised Him from the dead, you will be saved."***
***Romans10:9***

# ABOUT THE CONTRIBUTORS:

***Aurora Ileto Opiniano*** *is a Certified Public Accountant (CPA) in the Philippines, a Certified Management Accountant (CMA), and a Chartered Professional Accountant (CPA) in Canada. She was one of the speakers in the Empower Prayer - Atlantic Canada's Prayer Equipping & Summit held in Nova Scotia in June 2011, where she shared the topic "Devotion." She was born in the Philippines and married with four children and five grandchildren (and counting). Her journey with the Lord began when she accepted Jesus Christ as her Lord and Savior on September 13, 1981. Her family immigrated to Canada in October 1994, holding on to God's promise in the book of Joshua 1:8-9 "...Have I not commanded you? Be strong and of good courage; do not be afraid, nor be dismayed, for the Lord your God is with you wherever you go." Her favorite verse in the Bible is Isaiah 40:31. She is cancer and covid survivor.*

***Edith Arabe Fadul -*** *Edith is the youngest of 6 children and blessed with the privilege to care for their parents, Martin and Nina, both exceptional in their respective fields. Edith is a redeemed sinner. She aspires to be the best version for her Saviour, Jesus Christ. Edith has 30 years of experience in banking and initially served in a USAID Project. She graduated from Legarda Elementary School, Philippine Science High School, the University of the Philippines, and the Asian Institute of Management. Edith continues conducting risk management workshops, mentoring, volunteering, and writing to encourage. Edith wrote Love in* *a Pandemic (2020), Thankful a Millionfold (2021), Choices, Chocolates, and Confidence: A Woman's Journey (2022) and RISK: Disaster or Opportunity? (2022). Edith's strength themes (Clifton methodology) are Learner (energized by the steady and deliberate journey to competence), Connectedness (believes all are part of a larger picture, a bridge-builder), Maximizer (focuses on strengths to stimulate personal and group excellence), Achiever (has a great deal of stamina and works hard), and Belief (has certain unchanging core values which define purpose in life).*

***Greva Garcia** (January 1969 - February 2011) was a loving wife to Edison and a mother to Miguel and Renzo. Her battle with cancer started in 2003 and gone to be with the Lord after eight years at age 42. She has been an inspiration in sharing her faith, and even in her struggle, she managed to share the Gospel and give Bibles to those around her. True to what was written on her epitaph, "I have fought the good fight, I have finished the race, I have kept the faith." 2 Timothy 4:7*

***Ian Opiniano** is a Graduate of Tyndale University, he is married to Fae Sanchez and blessed with three children. In 1994, at age four, he and his family immigrated to Canada. After 19 years, he attended the Youth With A Mission (YWAM) program in New Zealand and led a Mission trip in the Philippines (Olongapo, Tuguegarao, and Zambales City). Right now, he is the Pastor of Pluslife Church.*

***Marvin Jackson** (April 1949 - August 2015) &*
***Elaine Jackson** (November 1949 – February 2021)*

*They were wonderful husband and loving wife, both faithful servants of God. Marvin was a US veteran, a Pastor, and the Director of the ABA Disaster Relief Ministries, while Elaine loved to sing, play piano, and served in the church.*

***Milagros Cham Nava*** *is a widow, married to Nick, who became a pastor after 30 years of corporate life. She has three wonderful adult kids. Her breathtaking personal relationship with the Lord began July 18, 2003, when she accepted Jesus in her heart as Lord and Saviour. Her powerful encounters with the Lord keep her in awe of God's love, goodness, and grace, and she is all the hungrier for God's Presence. With the Lord, there is always more. Jesus is the greatest Lover of her soul. She shares God everywhere she goes, whether praying for, prophesying over, encouraging family, friends, and strangers, doing prayer walks, or conducting bible studies in her workplace, home, or church. She wants people to know and experience God like she does and more. She is now serving the Lord through the prayer team and discipleship ministries. She has 42 years of audit and compliance experience, 34 of which were in the banking industry.*

***Milagros Palad Gonzalvo*** *happily served the Lord together with her late husband, Pastor Alfredo Gonzalvo Sr. They started eleven mission churches in North, South, and Central Luzon in the Philippines from 1994-2007. She has three children and six grandchildren. She is a dressmaker who loves to sing, compose songs, and write poems. Her favorite Bible verse is Matthew 11:28: "Come to Me, all you who labor and are heavy laden, and I will give you rest."*

***Myrna Roman*** *is a publisher/blogger of Enjoying Wonderful World, a website about lifestyle, technology, entertainment, travel, and advocacy. She also contributes to several magazines and regional publications, is a freelancer PR, and is an Events and Media Coordinator. As part of her valuable work experience, she was an Admin head of an advertising company for a few years and a finance admin of a PR company for six years. She is a survivor of a brain aneurysm. She is a mother of four kids and a grandma to four wonderful grandchildren, and four fur babies (dogs).*

***Perry Requina*** *He studied at Bethel Bible College and Asia Pacific Theological Seminary. He became the Pastor of several churches in the Philippines. He and his family of six immigrated to Canada in 2008. He then studied at Trios and worked at Teen Challenge as an addiction worker.*

***Ritche O. Olivares*** *is a registered Social Worker. She is the Executive Director of Home of Hope, Inc. Ritche is the fifth child in the family of four brothers and one sister. Ritche has been a volunteer Sunday school teacher in her local Bible-believing church for over two decades. Ritche is a Social Worker by profession. The Lord has entrusted her to manage a Christian child-caring institution, "Home of Hope, Inc.", an orphanage in Bacolod City, for 39 years (and going).*

***Susana Fadul Roco*** *was born in November 1950 as the first grandchild in a large family. Born to quality parents, she is a quality Manila public school system product. She initially went to the University of Santo Tomas but transferred to Ramon Magsaysay HS and graduated Valedictorian. This got her into UP Diliman, where she earned her Bachelor in Secondary Education and her Masters in Art of Teaching with High Honors. She taught high school, undergraduate, and graduate courses at the UP System. She served as Asst. Dean at the Pamantasan Ng Maynila for a couple of years. At the Department of Education, Culture and Sports Philippines, she had the opportunity to make dramatic changes at the former Bureau of Non-Formal Education. She retired as Assistant Chief of the Literacy Division. She had to leave her two daughters when she immigrated to the USA with her husband. She enjoyed working in the Bay Area as a preschool teacher, the last one being in a Baptist mission school. After over a decade, her two daughters are now with her, also enjoying the benefits of US citizenship. She became a widow in 2021. Susana acknowledges God's Holy Spirit has always been with her and attributes all the highlights of her life to God's blessings!*

***Wilma Requina*** *(June 1963 - September 2022) was a woman of faith, a prayer warrior, a worshipper, and a servant of the Lord. She was Perry's beloved soulmate and the loving mama of four children. A fashionista who loved to sing, dance, laugh, hug, and share her time and talent in baking, jewelry making, and scrapbooking. She has an infectious laugh, a radiant smile, and a vibrant and happy disposition. Every moment was captured and remembered in her thousands of pictures. Very much loved by many, she had been a light and a salt that brought hope and joy to the people around her.*

# RESOURCES:

The Holy Bible (NKJV)

www.biblegateway.com

www.biblestudytools.com

www.israelmyglory.org

www.promisebiblestudy.com

www.wikipedia.org

Manufactured by Amazon.ca
Bolton, ON

37455604R00066